GOLFING

A View Through the Golf Hole

LEE H. VAN DAM

LHVD Books!
Lee H. Van Dam

Art by Emily E. Ferguson

Book design by Rebecca Hayes
www.beckypublisher.com

Published in the United States by
LHVD Books
Sandy, Utah
www.lhvdbooks.com

ISBN: 978–0–9903610–2–2

Library of Congress Control Number 2015920922

Also by the author –

Cruising – A View Through the Porthole

Contents

1 Addressing the Ball 1
2 Queuing Up at the Old Course 7
3 It's in the Cup 15
4 The "Ests" of Golf Courses 23
5 Did the Dutch Actually Invent Golf? 31
6 It's in the Record Book Only If… 37
7 Golf – The Babe's True Passion 43
8 "Gouff" in the Year 1527 49
9 Pantone 342 55
10 "Señor, I Think Your Ball Is in the Jungle!" 61
11 De Zwanen Regel *(The Swan Rule)* 67
12 10,000 Hours of Deliberate Golf Practice 75
13 Just Add Dimples 81
14 Midnight Madness Golf 87
15 Are Golfers Athletes? 93
16 Psst… Wanna Buy Some Golf Clubs? 99
17 Grandpa's Golf Gizmo 107
18 Practice Makes Permanent 119
19 How's Your Local Muni Doing? 127
20 Mission Hills 216 in China 135
21 Playing by Whose Rules? 141
22 The Road Less Traveled 147
23 Inside the Floating Green 151
24 Trees are 90% Air? Baloney! 159
25 My Personal Favorites 165
About the Author 169

1

Addressing the Ball

A favorite TV sitcom from years ago was *The Honeymooners,* starring Jackie Gleason. The episode called **"The Golfer"** that first aired on **October 15, 1955** has been ranked as one of the top ten sitcom episodes of all time. (Another one in the top ten that you're probably familiar with is Lucille Ball's 1952 candy factory episode where Lucy and Ethel try wrapping chocolates on a moving conveyor belt that keeps increasing in speed.) In the *Honeymooners* episode, Ralph Kramden (played by Gleason) and his best pal, Ed Norton (played by Art Carney), are in Ralph's apartment and they have a big problem. Ralph has been pretending at work that he is an expert golfer in order to get a promotion. **But Ralph doesn't actually know how to play golf, and when his boss invites him to join him for a round, Ralph is in a pickle.**

So Norton gets out a big golf instruction book and tries to give Ralph a golf lesson. Ralph shows up in the kitchen of the apartment for the lesson wearing outrageous plaid knicker pants, argyle socks, an ugly patterned sweater, and a hilarious tam o' shanter golf hat with a toorie pom pom in the center. Ralph has one golf club, an old wooden driver, but no ball, so Ed gets out a pin cushion that still has pins in it to use as a ball. They then proceed with the lesson.

A highlight of the episode is when Norton, reading from the instruction book, tells Ralph that the first thing he needs to do is to step up, plant his feet firmly on the ground, and **"address the ball."** Ralph gives Ed one of his patented *Honeymooners* glares and asks him what in the world it means to address the ball. Norton, not having any idea, takes the club, steps up to the ball, plants his feet, looks at the ball, and says, **"Hellooooo ball!"** (The entire episode is available on YouTube, as is the Lucille Ball one. I highly recommend both of them.)

Whether it is addressing the ball, or whatever we choose to do with it, the golf ball itself is a most interesting part of the game of golf. **The golf ball has been studied, analyzed, tested, compared, and redesigned more than any other ball in sports.** There are many interesting facts and numerous bits of information about golf balls. Let's look at just a few of them:

- It has been estimated that at any given time on any given day **there is at least one golf ball up in the air somewhere in the world.**
- The fastest–moving ball in all of sports is a golf ball with a top recorded speed of **204 miles per hour.** The second fastest is a pelota, the goatskin–covered ball used in the sport of jai alai. It has been measured at 188 mph.
- Golf balls require **more steps in the manufacturing process** than any other sports ball.
- **Golf balls travel farther on hot days.** For each 25°F increase in air temperature, the ball will go an additional eight to ten yards. And, of course, they also travel farther at higher altitudes.
- Studies say that **the most visible golf balls** in order of ease of spotting them are **(1) yellow, (2) white, (3) orange, and (4) pink.** Yellow balls are said to be about three times easier to see than white balls at a distance of 250 yards.
- **There are over 130 games or sports that involve the**

use of a ball, with golf balls being among the smallest of all the sports balls used in these games. Only several others, such as squash balls and table tennis balls, are smaller in size than a golf ball.

- **A golf ball will float in the Dead Sea.** A regulation golf ball will sink in fresh water and in the ocean – but it will float in the Dead Sea. And it will sometimes float in the Great Salt Lake. The salinity of the Great Salt Lake varies from year to year and it also varies in different parts of the lake, and so a golf ball will sometimes float in the lake and sometimes it will not.
- The highest price at auction ever paid for a golf ball was **$55,865** for a ball autographed by Bobby Jones.
- Golf balls have the distinction **of being lost more than any other ball in sports – by a huge margin!**
- The U.S. patent office has granted **over 5,000 patents for golf balls.**
- **There are two golf balls sitting on the moon.** Alan Shepard never retrieved the two balls he hit there on February 6, 1971.
- **The driving of golf balls off the back of cruise ships has been banned.** The Marpol V international treaty

> (Marpol stands for marine pollution) prohibits the dumping of plastic and plastic–type items, including golf balls, from ships at sea. However, several companies are developing biodegradable golf balls that would be considered permissible to use under the treaty.

And concerning the phrase **"addressing the ball," it is an actual term used in the official Rules of Golf.** It means to step up to the ball, take your stance, and prepare to hit the ball. Addressing the ball is a critical action in golf because if a player's ball in play moves after it has been addressed (other than as a result of a stroke), **the player incurs a penalty of one stroke** – unless it is obvious that an outside force such as a gust of wind moved it.

Golf Term

Sabbath Sticks

Sabbath sticks were old golf clubs disguised as walking sticks or canes – and sometimes even as umbrellas. In the 1800s, because playing golf on Sunday was frowned on by the Church of Scotland, some avid golfers made or obtained walking sticks with a small golf club–type head on one end. The small wood or iron head fit in the palm of the hand and was virtually unnoticeable as the golfer strolled to church with the aid of the cane. **After church services, the golfer would take the long way home, playing a little golf along the way with his Sabbath stick, hitting stones, acorns, or even a golf ball he had hidden in his coat.**

2

Queuing Up at the Old Course

Despite having to queue up twice, **Tuesday, September 3, 2002** was a truly wonderful day in my life. **That was the day I played golf at the Old Course in St. Andrews** and also did several other memorable things in Scotland. It was one of those days that makes life very special.

I mention queuing up because it is such an interesting custom in Great Britain. To queue up is to line up, but not just like the rest of the world does, but to do so in a most formal and serious manner. British people queue up a lot. **It is a long–standing tradition that is even governed by rules of etiquette.** The following are excerpts from the booklet *English Manners* (author unknown):

- A proper British citizen queues correctly and politely. It is the right thing to do.
- Be patient and don't get cross. Queuing is about fair play. Remember that everyone in the queue is in the same circumstance.

- Respect the personal space of others. There is no need to stand body–to–body in a queue. Doing so will only irritate people and may heighten an already fractious situation.
- If you are with several people, enter the queue as one group.
- Do not jump the queue! There are few things more likely to raise the ire of the British temperament than cutting the queue.

The British even enjoy poking fun at themselves about queues, according to the June 2013 issue of *Great Britain Magazine*:

- A person from Great Britain, even if he is alone, forms an orderly queue of one.
- Napoleon said the British were a nation of shopkeepers, but we really are more a nation of queuers.
- According to the Telegraph, the average Brit spends at least six months of their life queuing.

- The time we spend waiting in queues during our daily lives is almost as interesting to us as the weather. After discussing the weather, a fascination with queuing is our second most popular trait.
- We British love our traditions – the Queen, roast dinner, double–decker buses, fish and chips, and queuing.
- It has been said that Britain would win an automatic gold medal if queuing became an Olympic sport.
- Many Brits find queuing magnetic and will join the end of one just to see what is at the front.

My wife and I arrived in St. Andrews after taking a few days to drive up from London in a rental car. Driving on the opposite side of the road was a real adventure, especially after negotiating the many roundabouts and then trying to remember which side of the upcoming street we were supposed to be on. We arrived at our quaint Bed & Breakfast in St. Andrews **(the wonderful Aslar Guest House)** on Monday afternoon. After checking in we spent the rest of the day looking around the interesting town with its many sights and shops. We visited the grounds of the University of St. Andrews, the oldest university in Scotland, (where Prince William and Duchess Kate went to school and where they met each other) and **paid homage to both Old Tom Morris and Young Tom Morris** who are buried in the cemetery by the old St. Andrews Cathedral. (Old and Young Tom each won four British Open Championships.) We then had a bite to eat, went back to the guest house, set the alarm clock for 5:00 a.m., and went to bed.

I awoke at 4:55 a.m. and after a three–minute walk down the street and around a corner, I was at the Old Course. By 5:10 a.m. I was **queued up** at the starter's box (a small building near the first tee) **where I was #5 in the queue.** It was a beautiful sunny morning with just a slight breeze. No rain was expected. Within a few minutes there were another 20–25 golfers queuing up behind me. At the Old Course, it is difficult to get tee times and often your best chance of getting on the course is to arrive early as a single golfer and to queue up.

Queuing up turned out to be a lot of fun. We chatted with the starter who was a well–weathered and colorful Scottish gentleman, dressed in tweed, who spoke a brand of English I could hardly recognize. He took down our names, checked our handicap cards (males with a handicap higher than 24 and females higher than 36 are not allowed to play on the Old Course), and advised us to be very patient because the course was fully–booked for the day and he had no idea if any of us would be able to get out. He then put on quite a show as he began telling us wonderful old stories about golf at St. Andrews.

Several groups teed off while we were waiting – **and then a wonderful thing happened.** The 7:20 a.m. foursome didn't show up! The starter called queuers #1 through #4, but #1 and #2 had left the queue for a few minutes to look at the old club house, **so the starter indicated that #3, #4, #5, and #6 should prepare themselves immediately to tee off. Wow, I had made it!**

Standing on the **first tee** brought chills. There I was at the Old Course, the place that has played such a major role in golf. I felt it was a real privilege to be there. My first tee shot was a pretty good one, and my second shot made it onto the first green without going into the meandering little stream, **the Swilcan Burn,** that guards the front of the putting surface. My par putt lipped the cup and I was happy to take a bogey on the hole. With my jitters now gone, playing each succeeding hole was a great thrill. I especially remember:

- The par–five **5th hole** with its **seven hidden bunkers** positioned out where most tee shots land.
- **Hole #11,** a 174–yard par three that can play anywhere from **a 3–iron to a 9–iron depending on the wind.**
- The **14th hole** with the fearsome **Hell bunker,** which is deeper than I am tall and which my ball landed in.
- **The Road Hole, #17,** where your drive has to clear **the wall of the hotel** and then land on a fairway that isn't visible from the tee. I missed the fairway.

And then I came to the **18th tee box.** In front of me was a beautiful panorama made up of the wide finishing fairway, the famous **Swilcan Bridge** (one of the best photo ops in all of golf), and the majestic **Royal & Ancient clubhouse** in the background. And in front of the difficult undulating green 357 yards away sat the treacherous **Valley of Sin,** a deep swale where many championships have been lost. I tried my best, but my second shot hit the upslope in front of the green, trickled backwards, and ended up in the deep depression. It took me several additional shots to get the ball in the cup, and although I didn't par the hole, I finished the round with a big smile on my face and with tremendous appreciation for the Old Course and for the game of golf. I felt truly blessed to be part of all of that.

And the day wasn't even over yet! My wife met me by the 18th green where we took photos, and then we strolled to the **Old Course Hotel** and had a pleasant lunch at a table overlooking the golf course. We then headed back towards the old part of town where we found a neat old golf shop, **Auchterlonies,** which has been making clubs since 1895. The proprietor was most helpful. I was looking for some old golf memorabilia, and he allowed us to rummage around in their old, dusty shop and storage area at the rear of the building. We found several wonderful vintage clubs, some very old golf balls, and an old, slender, well–used canvas and leather golf bag large enough for just a few clubs. We negotiated a satisfactory price and now all those items are on display in my office. I can see them from my desk as I write this chapter.

Back at the guest house we rested up for a while and then drove a short distance to **West Sand**, the famous beach that was the setting for the opening of ***Chariots of Fire***. You may recall the scene where the camera follows a group of runners jogging along the sand while the movie's famous theme music by **Vangelis** plays in the background. Holly took pictures of me while I ran on the beach – minus the theme music. We then headed a few miles south of St Andrews to the little village of **Anstruther**, located on the Firth of Forth, where they say Scotland's best fish and chips shop is located. It was dinner time at the **Anstruther Fish Bar**, so we **queued up** with everyone else who had come to try their famous food. The delicious fish and chips were well worth the lengthy wait.

So, that's how **Tuesday, September 3, 2002** went for me – **queuing up** for golf at the Old Course, buying several old golf clubs at Auchterlonies, running on West Sand, and **queuing up again** to eat Scotland's best fish and chips at the Anstruther Fish Bar. It was one of the most memorable days in my life!

(Note – If you'd like to read an interesting book about golfing at the Old Course, I'd recommend *An American Caddie in St. Andrews*, by Oliver Horovitz.)

Golf Term

Chili Dip (Also called a Hormel)

Chili dipping a shot is pretty embarrassing, but it is not that uncommon. **To chili dip is to mishit a chip shot by hitting the ground behind the ball before contacting the ball itself.** The result is a weak shot in which the ball doesn't move very far. This kind of mishit can also be called **a Hormel, hitting it fat, or chunking the ball.**

When eating Mexican food, to chili dip is to scoop up some chili with a tortilla chip. And when you chili dip a golf shot, you scoop up dirt and grass in front of the ball with your club face while barely making contact with the ball.

The first use of the term chili dip as it applies to golf seems to be of fairly recent origin, going back to tournament golf in the **mid–1970s** when golf announcers began using it in order to add color and interest to their TV broadcasts.

And just in case you're wondering, I checked it out and Hormel Foods currently makes 14 types of canned chili. I love chili when I'm camping and my favorite type is Hormel Chunky Chili with Beans. **The company was started in 1891 by George A. Hormel who was an avid golfer and founder and first president of the Austin Country Club in Austin, Minnesota.** George died in 1946, several decades before his company's name became associated with this unfortunate golf shot – **the chili dip.**

It's in the Cup

"While you are at Hogwarts, your triumphs will earn you house points, while any rule–breaking will lose house points. At the end of the year, the house with the most points is awarded the **House Cup,** a great honor."
– Professor Minerva McGonagall, *Harry Potter and the Sorcerer's Stone*

The winning house at Hogwarts receives the **House Cup**; the winner of the Canadian Football League championship game takes home the **Grey Cup**; **America's Cup** is the prize in the premier yachting competition in the world; the **World Cup** (the most widely–watched sporting event on earth) is awarded every four years to the best football country in the world; the **Ryder Cup** goes to the best team in a biennial international golf competition; and the **Stanley Cup** (surely one of the grandest of all the cups) is given to the winner of the National Hockey League playoffs.

Why are cups given as trophies to so many sports winners? When and where did this tradition begin?

After battles in the Middle Ages, the triumphant soldiers needed something to take back home to show tangible proof of their victory. **Pieces of armor, or perhaps an occasional body part, were the trophies they won and displayed.** In Spain, the successful matador would be given one of the bull's ears as his trophy. And in sporting competitions, winners were often awarded with land or money – or eventually something of value they could put on display, **something such as a nice, shiny cup.** To make it easier to give, receive, and carry, handles (ears) were often affixed to the sides of the cups.

Golf has embraced the idea of giving cups to the winners of golf tournaments. Here's a sampling of several of the cups associated with golf:

- **Ryder Cup** – This beautiful gold cup with a golfer on top is awarded to the winner of a golf competition held every two years between teams from Europe and the USA. One of my favorite golf events to watch, **the Ryder Cup makes for great TV and is always an amazingly intense competition.** The event is named after the English businessman, Samuel Ryder, who sponsored the first event and donated the trophy. Himself an avid golfer, Ryder made his fortune by originating the idea of selling small packets of garden seeds through the mail.

- **Presidents Cup** – This match play competition is similar to the Ryder Cup, but the two teams are the USA and an international team from the rest of the world, minus Europe. The event has 34 matches compared to 28 for the Ryder Cup. The head of state from the location of the previous Presidents Cup is chosen as the honorary chairperson for each biennial competition. Past honorary chairpersons have been Thabo Mbeki, president of South Africa, in 2005; George W. Bush in 2007; Stephen Harper, prime minister of Canada, in 2009; Barack Obama in 2011 and 2015; and Julia Gillard, prime minister of Australia, in 2013. No prize money is awarded to the players. **Instead, the net proceeds of the tournament are distributed to charities nominated by the players.** The Presidents Cup trophy is a large 28–pound vermeil cup made by Tiffany & Company. (Vermeil is a combination of sterling silver and gold – 24–karat gold in this case.)
- **Solheim Cup** – The Solheim Cup is the women's version of the Ryder Cup and is played using the same team setup and format. The brainchild of Karsten Solheim, this competition between the USA and Europe is played over three days with each team having 12 players. You might remember what made Karsten Solheim famous. Originally a shoemaker, he was the one who re–engineered the putter, moving the shaft more towards the center of the club head instead of keeping it back on the heel of the club. **The result was the Ping putter,** a club that made an interesting "ping" sound when it hit the ball. (I still have and treasure my old Ping putter.) The trophy for the winning team is a gorgeous Waterford crystal cup valued in excess of $50,000. It is 19 inches tall and weighs over 20 pounds.
- **Walker Cup** – Named after **George Herbert Walker** who was President George H. W. Bush's (#41) grandfather and President George W. Bush's (#43) great–grandfather, the Walker Cup is the original international

golf competition that spawned the others. (The connection to the Bush family came about when George Herbert Walker's daughter, Dorothy, married Prescott Bush.) In 1920, George Herbert Walker was the president of the United States Golf Association. He proposed that the leading male **amateur** golfers of the USA compete against the best male **amateur** golfers of England, Ireland, Scotland, and Wales every two years on alternating sides of the Atlantic. He provided a trophy for the winners of the event, which originally was called, "The United States Golf Association International Challenge Trophy." **The press had a problem with the lengthy name and just called it the Walker Cup.** Although Walker balked at having it bear his name, it stuck. Today's Walker Cup trophy is a huge silver cup with unusually large ears. At first the USA dominated the amateur competition, but since 1989 it has been quite even with the USA team winning seven Walker Cups compared to six for the Great Britain and Ireland team.

- **The Claret Jug** – The Claret Jug is a beautiful, tall, slender cup with just one handle. It is the trophy given to the winner of the prestigious Open Championship (the British Open). The original jug dates back to 1872. It cost £20 (twenty British pounds) to purchase at that time and was made by Mackay Cunningham & Company of Edinburgh, Scotland. **Many feel that this cup is the ultimate prize in golf.**
- **Fightmaster Cup** – Sponsored by the Society of One–armed Golfers and patterned after the Ryder Cup, the Fightmaster Cup is an interesting match play tournament for teams from North America and Europe. **All the participants are one–armed golfers!** The competition is named after Don Fightmaster who has been dubbed "the Arnold Palmer of the one–armed golf world." After losing his left arm in an accident, Don has gone on to win a number of tournaments for disabled golfers and has inspired numerous people with permanent disabilities to

take up the game of golf. The golfers who compete for the Fightmaster Cup are amazing golfers. The cup presented to the winning team is an artistic–looking silver trophy with a one–armed golfer on top.

Golf is proud of these cups, as well as the many cups that we haven't mentioned here that are awarded to the winners of other golf contests. **In my mind, beautiful cups are wonderfully–appropriate rewards for excellence in golf and other sporting events** and I especially like the fact that so many of them have such interesting and long histories.

Besides cups and the other typical things presented to sports winners, there also are a number of unusual or even odd trophies that we might mention:

- A full–size **silver–plated milk can** is presented to the winner of the annual Boise State vs. Fresno State college football game.
- **The Ashes Urn,** which contains the charred remnants of a burned cricket ball, is the small 4.5–inch terracotta trophy given to the winner of the England vs. Australia test series in cricket.
- From 1930 to 1943, the winner of the Minnesota vs. Wisconsin football game was the custodian for the year of the **Slab of Bacon Trophy.**
- A carved wooden turtle named **Illibuck** is given to the Illinois vs. Ohio State football game winner.
- And the **Keg of Nails Trophy,** a replica of an old keg used to hold ordinary construction nails, goes to the winner of the Louisville vs. Cincinnati game.

And at each Van Dam family reunion, the winning team in our traditional **egg toss contest** receives a homemade traveling trophy representative of our family's Dutch heritage. **We call it the "ei trophy" (ei is Dutch for egg).** The trophy is made up of two small wooden shoes, a miniature windmill, some plastic tulips, a commemorative metal reunion button, a Dutch doll, an empty can of Dutch soup, and a stroopwafel (a Dutch syrup cookie) all mounted on an old remnant of wood with pieces of egg shell glued to the top.

Like the Hogwarts House Cup is to Harry Potter and the sports cups are to sports winners, the Van Dam egg toss trophy is a prized and honored possession in the Van Dam family.

Golf Term

Condor

What does a **condor**, the largest flying land bird in the Western Hemisphere, have to do with golf? Well, let's see. A **birdie** is getting one under par on a hole. An **eagle** is two under par. An **albatross** is three. **And when you get four under par on a single hole it is a condor.** (Or, four under par on a hole is sometimes called a triple eagle or a double albatross, although the math really doesn't quite work for these if you think about it.) **A condor is what you get if you hit a hole–in–one on a par 5 hole.** Has it ever happened? Yes, it has. There are several instances of golfers getting condors – but none of those took place in a pro tour event. **A condor is considered to be the rarest feat in all of golf.**

1 under par – birdie
2 under par – eagle
3 under par – albatross
4 under par – condor

A condor (the feathered animal) can have a wing span up to 10 feet. And the type of condor found in North America, the California Condor, is quite rare, being on the **endangered species list.** Native Americans consider the California Condor to be sacred.

4

The "Ests" of Golf Courses

When I wrote the book ***Cruising – A View Through the Porthole***, I included a chapter (Chapter #12) about the **"ests"** of cruise ships. That chapter listed and discussed such things as the newest cruise ships, the largest ships, the fastest ships, and the highest–rated ships. **In that same spirit, here is a chapter about the "ests" of golf courses.** There are **over 34,000** golf courses in the world, with about half of them being in the U.S. In second place is the United Kingdom with 8% of the total followed by Japan and Canada with 7% each.

Highest–Rated

The well–respected magazine, *Golf Digest,* lists these three as the highest–rated golf courses in the world:

#1 – Augusta National Golf Club, Augusta, Georgia
#2 – Pine Valley Golf Club, Pine Valley, New Jersey
#3 – Cypress Point Club, Pebble Beach, California

Longest and Largest

Longest Yardage: Jade Dragon Snow Mountain Golf Club, Lijang, China.

Nestled in the foothills of the Himalayas at an elevation of 10,800 feet, this course runs an incredible **8,548 yards.** Oxygen canisters and masks are provided in the golf carts for players who may feel light headed from the altitude.

Longest Entire Golf Course: Nullarbor Links, Australia.

From the 1st tee to the 18th green, this course runs **848 miles in length.** With a hole situated in each of 18 towns or roadhouses, this course spans two time zones. The course runs along a desolate highway (the Eyre Highway) **from Kalgoorlie in Western Australia to Ceduna in South Australia.** Golfers pick up a score card at the first city, play that hole, get a verification stamp, and then head out on the highway to the next town. On average, there is a distance of 47 miles between each of the 18 cities. Golfers typically take **at least four days** to complete the 18 holes.

Longest Golf Hole: Hole #3, Gunsan Country Club, Gunsan, South Korea.

Playing **1,097 yards** from the tips, this par 7 hole is nearly 11 football fields long (0.62 of a mile). To hit the green in regulation (that is, to make it onto the green in 5 shots) you **just hit your driver and then four fairway woods in a row.** Easy.

Largest Bunker: Hell's Half Acre, Pine Valley Golf Club, Pine Valley, New Jersey.

This gigantic bunker, located on the par five 7th hole, is said to be the largest one in the game. To be more technically correct, Hell's Half Acre is **the largest non–seaside bunker in the world** on a regulation golf course.

Geographic "Ests"

Farthest North: Ulukhaktok Golf Course, Ulukhaktok, Northwest Territories, Canada.

Located at **70°44' north latitude,** it lies off the Amundsen Gulf in the Beaufort Sea. Animals often seen on the course are caribou, musk oxen, polar bears, and wolves.

Farthest South: Ushuaia Golf Course, Tierra del Fuego, Argentina.

At **54°48' south latitude,** it is at the very tip of South America in a region known as "the end of the world." I played there several years ago and found it to be a very nice course. The area averages 160 days of rain or snow per year.

Highest Elevation: Yak Golf Club, Kupup, East Sikkim, India.

This 18–hole layout is part of an Indian Army base at **13,025 feet above sea level.** Yaks are available to rent for golfers to ride on – **and the yak's saddle includes a place where you can attach your golf bag.** The club's website says, "A golfer, unless acclimatized to these majestic heights, needs to move slowly on the course. Yaks are recommended to be used by senior members." Certificates are given to golfers to verify that they have played the very highest course in the world. (Note: The highest golf course used to be the Tuctu Golf Club in Morococha, Peru at 14,335 feet above sea level, but it has been abandoned for several years.)

Lowest Elevation: Furnace Creek Golf Course, Death Valley, California.

At **214 feet below sea level,** this is a good one to play really early in the morning. That's what I did in July several years ago on a day when the temperature reached 120° later in the afternoon. My round of golf that day was **my lowest ever,** of course. Furnace Creek hosted an annual golf tournament called the Heatstroke Open until a few years ago.

Coldest: Uummannaq Golf Course, Uummannaq, Greenland.

Laid out on shelf ice, this is the home to the World Ice Golf Championship. Golfers play orange balls and are cautioned against using clubs with graphite shafts which can become brittle and break in the super–cold temperatures reaching **more than 30° below zero.** Because of the shifting ice, the shape and layout of the course changes from year to year.

Other Golf Course "Ests"

Hardest: The Ocean Course, Kiawah Island, South Carolina.

Long, windy, and known for its treacherous bunkers and slick greens, this course is a classic Pete Dye design. Famous for his extremely difficult layouts, Dye designed this course with the most seaside holes (10) of any golf course in North America. The Ocean Course has **the highest combination of course rating (79.6) and slope rating (155)** of any course in the world.

Most Unusual: Prison View Golf Course, Louisiana State Penitentiary, Angola, Louisiana.

The entirety of this course lies within a maximum security prison, the largest adult male maximum security prison in the U.S. with over 5,000 inmates. The golf course is open to prison employees and the public, but not to prisoners. **A background check is required at least 48 hours before playing golf.** The tee markers are handcuffs welded shut and painted white, and a local rule warns the golfers that play may be suspended at any time due to institutional needs or at the warden's discretion. Souvenir T–shirts at a nearby gift shop show a picture of the prison and say, **"Angola, A Gated Community."**

Biggest Change in Tee to Green Elevation: The Legend Golf & Safari Resort, Limpopo, South Africa.

This course has an optional 19th hole called **The Extreme 19th**, which is said to be the toughest par 3 on the planet. If you choose to play it, a helicopter takes you to the tee on Hanglip Mountain, **1,300 feet above a green** that is shaped like the continent of Africa. Tracking equipment and four video cameras allow the golfers to follow the flight of their ball. It takes about **20 seconds** after teeing off for the ball to land. Pádraig Harrington was the first to get a par on the hole. Since then several birdies have been achieved, but no holes–in–one.

Most Dangerous: Camp Bonifas Golf Hole, Panmunjom, Korea.

This "course" is a single par three golf hole located near the **Korean Demilitarized Zone,** the most fortified border in the world. At a length of 192 yards, it is bordered on three sides by mine fields. The elevated tee box sits on top of an empty machine gun nest, with North Korea just a mulligan away. A sign at the tee says, **"Danger! Do not retrieve balls from the rough. Live mine fields."**

Well, there is the list of the golf course **"ests."** Now what I have to do is figure out a way to play all of these courses. That would be quite an adventure and a lot fun. As mentioned, I've had the chance to play two of them already – Ushuaia in Argentina and Furnace Creek in Death Valley. To get to the other ones I'll have to make up a plan, set aside quite a bit of travel time, save some money – and convince my wife that this is a good thing to do. And I do see a bit of a problem concerning playing at Augusta National. It is **a very private course** where only guests invited by members are allowed to play. **Do any of you readers happen to belong to**

Augusta National?

(Please note that the information in this chapter comes from a variety of sources including my own research, Wikipedia, various internet sites, the Guinness Book of World Records, and several golf publications. The lists are current as of the date of this book.)

Golf Term

"G" as in Golf

The NATO phonetic alphabet is the most widely–used spelling alphabet in the world. It is what we often hear in movies and TV shows when radio operators, airplane pilots, and others are spelling out a word to make sure that the person on the other end doesn't misunderstand it. For example, the code word for the letter "A" is Alfa, "B" is Bravo, "C" is Charlie – **and "G" is Golf.** "G" used to be represented by the word George – but not anymore. Now the word **Golf** is used instead. Here is why:

In the mid–1950s, after going through two world wars and the Korean conflict, **it was apparent that there needed to be a standardized phonetic alphabet system for worldwide use.** The problem was that the various systems in existence sometimes used different words for the letters of the alphabet and that some of the words being used were often mispronounced and misunderstood, especially by the speakers of some foreign languages.

After studying the situation and testing thousands of people from over 30 nationalities, **NATO developed a phonetic alphabet that now has been adopted by most countries and worldwide agencies.** Although generally known as the NATO phonetic alphabet, its official name is the International Radiotelephony Spelling Alphabet. Among other changes, this new phonetic alphabet dropped the word George and **instead used the word Golf to represent the letter "G".** Experts felt that the word **Golf** would be easier to pronounce and clearer to understand.

So now, using the NATO phonetic alphabet, if someone wishes to spell out the word **G–O–L–F** while piloting a plane or broadcasting on a ham radio, here is what they would say:

"G" as in Golf
"O" as in Oscar
"L" as in Lima
"F" as in Foxtrot

Did the Dutch Actually Invent Golf?

As mentioned previously, I have Dutch heritage. My great–grandfather was born in Heukelem, a tiny village in Holland, **and I am of the belief that the origin of the game of golf can be traced to The Netherlands rather than to Scotland.** Granted, Scotland bills itself as the home of golf, and I concede that it was in Scotland that the modern game was popularized and developed, **but before it was played in Scotland, history shows us, in literature and in art, that people in Holland were playing a game where they hit balls with sticks at targets and holes. And they called what they did colf.**

And what evidence is there of this?

- **Exhibit #1** – Exhibit #1 is an entry in the year 1261 where **Dutch/Flemish poet Jacob van Maerlant,** in a manuscript called *Boeck Merlyn*, mentioned that people in his village were playing a game with a ball and a club. The game was played with curved wooden clubs and round wooden balls in open fields around the towns, in the streets, and in the churchyards.

- **Exhibit #2** – My next evidence is **Loenen aan de Vecht.** Loenen aan de Vecht is a small village in Holland about 6 miles west of today's Hilversum where the Dutch played a game with a stick and a ball outside of the castle's gates. According to records written in 1297, whoever could hit the ball into a distant target with the fewest number of strokes was the winner of the game. On a recent trip to Holland, my wife and I drove to Loenen aan de Vecht and discovered that there still is a quaint village there – **and that just outside the village is a 9–hole golf course called Golfclub Old Course Loenen.** I didn't have my clubs with me, but I did have a small bag with several golf balls, tees, and a golf glove that I usually take with me when I travel. Two kind Dutch gentlemen near the first tee invited me to join them for golf and insisted I use some of their extra clubs instead of renting a set. **We had a great time playing on what they claimed was the first official golf course in the world.**

- **Exhibit #3** – In 1389, the regent of the city of Haarlem in The Netherlands donated to the citizens of his town a field called **"De Baen" (meaning the course)** which was located outside the city. It was to be used exclusively for playing games – especially the game called colf – because hitting the small hard balls around with a wooden club was considered to be too dangerous to be done within the city walls.
- **Exhibit #4** – And my final item of proof is the beautiful old painting by **Dutch artist Aert van der Neer** depicting Dutch people entertaining themselves by playing a game called kolven on a frozen canal with a windmill in the background. The painting is titled, "Sports on a Frozen River."

So it appears to me that prior to the time that the official game of golf was being developed in Scotland, a similar game with a similar name was already being played in The Netherlands.

Ian Morrison, an Australian journalist, put some perspective on the question about where golf was invented. He said:

> **"Unlike many other sports, golf does not enjoy the privilege of knowing its exact birthright."**

And golf is not alone in this. Often the person or persons who invented many of the things we use today is up for debate. For example:

- **The Airplane** – We give the Wright brothers the honor of being the inventors of the airplane. However, some say that in March 1903, some nine months before the Wright brothers' famous flight near Kitty Hawk, North Carolina, **a New Zealand farmer named Richard Pearse** flew some 350 yards in an aircraft before crashing into a hedge. Although he had several eyewitnesses present, there were no journalists there to record and publish the feat.

- **Gunpowder** – We all pretty well acknowledge that China gets the credit for inventing gunpowder, but exactly who in China came up with the idea and when did it happen? One story is that **an unknown Chinese cook in the 9th century** was experimenting with a new recipe in his kitchen and mixed charcoal, sulfur, and saltpeter together. All three of these ingredients were items commonly found in Chinese kitchens. As he added heat to the mixture, it all of a sudden exploded – and gunpowder was born.
- **The Automobile** – Although Michigan's Henry Ford perfected the art of making them on an assembly line, it was the German **Karl Benz** who probably should be given credit for the invention of the automobile, although there were others working on similar creations at the same time. But it was Benz in 1886 who received the very first patent for a vehicle fueled by gasoline and he is generally considered to be the father of the motor car.

But with certain other things, it is pretty clear who gets credit for the idea:

- **Instant Noodles** – Momofuku Ando of Japan in 1958 (today **95 billion** servings are eaten worldwide each year)
- **Legos Plastic Blocks** – Ole Kirk Christiansen of Denmark in 1949 (the name Lego comes from the Danish words leg godt, meaning play well)
- **7 Up** – Charles Leiper Grigg of the USA in 1929 (the drink was first called Bib–Label Lithiated Lemon–Lime Soda)
- **The Saxophone** – Adolphe Sax of Belgium in 1846 (he also invented the saxotromba, the saxhorn, and the saxtuba)

- **Chocolate Chip Cookies** – Ruth Wakefield of the USA in 1938 (The owner of the Toll House Inn in Massachusetts, she is said to have invented them by accident. They were originally called Toll House Crunch Cookies.)
- **WD–40** – Norm Larsen of the USA in 1953 (WD–40 is abbreviated from the phrase Water Displacement, 40th Formula)

When it comes right down to it, I guess it really doesn't matter much who gets the credit for coming up with a great new idea for a thing, a process, or a sport – **unless it pertains to golf and you are Dutch – and then it is critical to make sure history gives proper acknowledgement to the proper people.**

Golf Term

Divot

The word divot comes from Scotland in the 1500s. **A divot was a patch of grass that was dug out of the ground and placed on top of a house or shed as roofing material.** Over time golfers picked up on the term to describe the piece of turf dug up when a golfer hits an iron shot in a fairway. At first a divot referred only to the clump of grass itself. Eventually the hole that was left by the shot was also called a divot.

While searching the word divot online, I discovered that there is a small community named **Divot, Texas.** It is located 68 miles southwest of San Antonio. I expected to find that it got its name due to some connection to the game of golf. But that is not the case. It got its name by mistake. In 1910 a request was submitted to the government to build a post office in that area **and to name the community Pivot,** but due to poor penmanship on the application form, the suggested name was misread and **the community and its new post office were named Divot rather than Pivot.** No one objected to the error and no one had time to redo the application, so Divot was accepted – and the name stuck.

6

It's in the Record Book Only If…

If you are into sports, don't you just love all the statistics and records that are kept? I surely do. Baseball recognizes **Don Larsen** as the only person to pitch a perfect game in the World Series (game 5 of the 1956 Series); **Usain Bolt's** 9.58–second 100–meter dash in 2009 is the fastest ever; and **Wilt Chamberlain's** 100 points is the most scored by an individual player in an NBA game (1962, Philadelphia Warriors vs. New York Nicks).

Golf also loves its statistics and records. Golf courses and country clubs typically keep track of such things as who has shot the lowest round, what holes–in–one have been scored, and who the reigning club champion is. And especially in the world of professional golf, extensive records have been kept over many years in a large number of categories of achievement. **Looking only at professional golfers in PGA TOUR events,** here are several accomplishments that I found of particular interest:

It's in the Record Book Only If.....

How would you feel if you made your first hole–in–one in a professional tournament and it ended up not counting? Well, that's what happened in 1971 to Lee Trevino at the Tucson Open. **During the first round, Trevino aced the fourth hole by hitting his ball into the cup on the fly.** He finished the round at 72 – even par. But not everyone else was able to finish. A huge storm moved into the area and less than half of the other golfers had completed their round when tournament officials halted play. Later that day they decided to cancel the entire round, **thereby wiping out all scores, including Trevino's hole–in–one.** His ace doesn't appear in the books. It's like it never happened.

The next day the round was rescheduled and this time all the golfers were able to finish. Even though Lee Trevino didn't get credit for his hole–in–one made the day before, he wasn't as upset as he might have been because **in the rescheduled round he shot a three–under–par 69, three better than the previous day.** Oh, and did Lee Trevino ever ace another hole? Yes he did. The record book shows that in 1973 at the USI Classic he got his only official hole–in–one on the tour.

Highest Score on a Single Hole

As of this writing, this record is held by **John Daly**. Do you remember how it took place? In 1998, on the par–5 sixth hole at Bay Hill (a hole with a huge lake running along the side of it), **Daly hit six consecutive balls into the water and carded an 18 for the hole.** After the round, he was asked why he didn't just take a drop or aim for a nearer part of the fairway instead of continuing to try to hit balls over the water. His reply? **"I'm not ashamed of what I did. I wasn't going to quit… and I just didn't have the wisdom to bail out."** And to his credit, Daly went on to birdie the next hole.

And how about you? What is the highest score you've had on a hole? Me? I don't exactly recall. But I know it was a pretty big number.

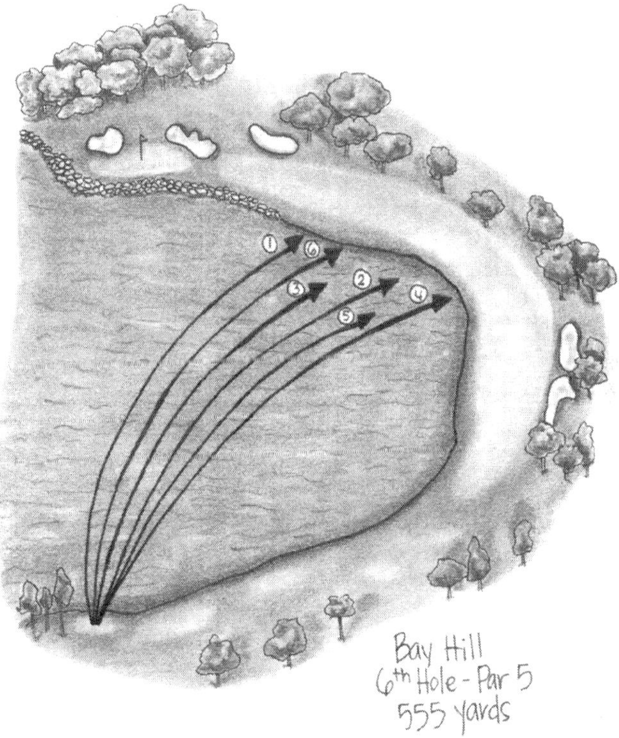

Number of Father and Son Combinations to Have Won PGA Events

To my thinking, this is one of the nicer statistics in golf. There have been nine fathers and sons win individual tournaments. Three of the nine pairs on this list are **Tom Morris, Sr. and his son, Tom Morris, Jr.; Craig Stadler and his son, Kevin Stadler; and Jay and Bill Haas. Jack Nicklaus and his son, Gary, came close to making the list,** but Gary Nicklaus never quite won a tour event. His best finish was in 2000 when he lost in a playoff to Phil Mickelson.

And here's something to think about. **How long before we have the combination of a father, a son, and a grandson win professional golf events?** I'm guessing it will happen sometime.

Most Consecutive Birdies in a Round

Mark Calcavecchia had **nine consecutive birdies** in the second round of the 2009 RBC Canadian Open. That is an all–time TOUR record. All nine of his birdie putts were from 15 feet or closer. His total score for that round of golf was 65 – and, interestingly, his caddie was his 15–year–old son, Eric. When asked after the round to comment on his achievement, Calc modestly replied, **"Records are made to be broken…It wouldn't surprise me if some guy whips out 10 birdies in a row sometime this weekend."** Well, so far it hasn't been done.

Note – As I was writing this up about Calc's achievement, I was curious about his son, Eric's, involvement in that round. I was able to send a note to Mark to ask him about it, and Mr. Calcavecchia was kind enough to give me the following reply:

"Lee, here are some answers to your questions. Eric was with me for two weeks mainly because he had nothing else to do in Arizona, so he came out to caddie…and he also caddied at the Buick the next week…so, yes, he looped all the rounds that week and the next. Luckily for me I didn't have to pay him anything other than room and board…and he eats a lot!!! During all the rain delays that one day I think he had the equivalent of about six full meals. He did help me read some putts, although if I didn't agree with him I went with what I thought. On Sunday, I wasn't making any putts so Eric says, 'Dad, why don't you use the birdie ball?' I just started laughing. I said that that ball had done its job and that it is going in my trophy room…and that I didn't want to take the chance of losing it." – Mark Calcavecchia

The most consecutive birdies I have ever had in one round on a regular golf course is three. How about you?

(Note – Special thanks to Laury Livsey and others at PGA TOUR headquarters for their help in providing information about PGA TOUR records.)

Golf Term

Stymie

From the Scottish word styme – meaning unable to see – stymie is an old golf term. It referred to a situation on a putting green where your opponent's golf ball was directly in the path (in the line) between your ball and the hole. **This left you stymied.** The rules of golf did not allow the opponent to mark and pick up their ball, so you had to putt around your opponent's ball – or even try to chip over it – in order to get your ball in the hole.

Now the word stymie is commonly used to mean to hinder, block, impede, or thwart, as in "Our competitor's patent stymied our ability to market a similar product."

Thank goodness that today's golf has a rule to prevent stymies. On the putting green it is now permissible, of course, to ask your opponent to mark and remove their ball if it is in or near your putt's line to the hole.

And as a side note, if you have ever played shuffleboard you know that a good defensive strategy is to purposely slide your disc so that it is in the way of your opponent's next shot. (My wife is an expert at doing this to me.) In the early days of golf, golfers sometimes would do a similar thing. **They would use their putt as a defensive ploy.** They would try to putt their ball so that it ended up between their opponent's ball and the hole, thus stymieing their opponent. **This is the only situation in golf that I am aware of that has ever allowed a golfer to take a defensive action against an opponent.**

Golf – The Babe's True Passion

One time when Holly and I were visiting Baltimore, we took the opportunity to go to the **birth home of Babe Ruth,** which is now an interesting museum. As one of the guides was explaining the exhibits to us, he pointed out a large photograph of Babe Ruth playing golf and mentioned that although The Babe loved playing baseball and was considered to be the greatest baseball player ever, **Babe Ruth's true passion was golf.**

I find it interesting that many great athletes are also avid golfers. Besides excelling at their particular professional sport, a large number of them are passionate about golf. Let's take a look at several athletes who are considered by many to be the all–time best in their sport to see what role golf has played in their lives.

Baseball – Babe Ruth

Babe Ruth had a remarkable baseball career. He hit 714 home runs, won 94 games as a pitcher, had a .342 lifetime batting average, and the teams he was on won seven World Series. Nearly every list of the greatest baseball players of all time puts Babe Ruth at the very top.

Babe Ruth was a member of the Leewood Country Club in Eastchester, New York. Commenting on the importance of golf in his life he said, **"I played 365 rounds of golf last year. Thank God for whoever invented golf. I'd be dead without it."** The story is told that a highway underpass near the Leewood golf course was built to provide a quicker route to Yankee Stadium so that The Babe could play golf as long as possible before he had to hurry away to arrive in time for that day's baseball game. In 1937, after his retirement, he won a tournament at his golf club, and guess what he did with the trophy they gave him? **He was so proud of it that he placed it in the area devoted to him in the Baseball Hall of Fame in Cooperstown, New York.**

Football – Jerry Rice

Jerry Rice, who was one of my favorite football players, is ranked #1 on many pro football all–time player lists. He has three Super Bowl rings and at the time of his retirement held **more than 36 all–time football records** (which is a record in itself). He picked up a love for golf while starting his football career with the San Francisco 49ers. It was common for Rice to begin and end his day on a golf course before and after football workouts. In a Golf Channel interview in 2013 he is quoted as saying, **"I devoted myself to football for over 25 years. I put my heart into it. And it is the same with golf."**

So how good a golfer is Jerry Rice? **Really good!** He is a scratch golfer, having a 0 handicap. (Actually, his official handicap is a bit better than 0. As of the writing of this book he carries a plus 0.7 handicap.) If one were to rank all currently–living pro athletes (who are not professional golfers) according to their golfing skills, Jerry Rice would be **among the top five.**

Basketball – Michael Jordan

Almost everyone is aware of Michael Jordan's love of golf. After all, he was the one who missed the ceremony to receive his first NBA Most Valuable Player award because he was playing back–to–back rounds of golf at Pinehurst at that time. Although he is not quite as good at golf as he was at basketball (he has a 1.2 golf handicap), he is passionate about playing the game and devotes many hours to it. He belongs to approximately 12 private golf clubs and owns more than 40 sets of clubs. In honor of his interest in golf, Nike even makes Air Jordan golf shoes. And once while visiting Disneyworld, **Jordan challenged Mickey Mouse to a putting contest.**

Jordan enjoys talking about his golf game and says that **one of his problems is consistency.** One day he'll be on top of his game only to follow it up with a bad round the next time he plays. He blames a lot of this on the mental aspect of golf. He says that on the basketball court he never thought about **"what if."** He just played basketball. But on the golf course he finds himself thinking about what might go wrong – like what might happen if his ball doesn't quite make it across the pond that lies in front of the green. He loves playing the game and says that he wants to get to the point where he can just enjoy it regardless of what happens. But he admits that his ultra–competitive attitude often gets in the way of allowing that to occur.

Boxing – Muhammad Ali

Muhammad Ali, who is considered to be the best boxer of all time, isn't much of a golfer. **Nevertheless, the man known as the Louisville Lip had plenty to say about the sport.** Some years ago Ali was being interviewed by Brad Wilson, a golf writer. Although Ali had hardly ever played golf, he told the reporter:

> **"Muhammad Ali is the world's greatest golfer!** Nobody can beat Muhammad Ali! Not Arnold Palmer! Not Jack Nicklaus! Not nobody! I'm gonna start with Arnold Palmer and Jack Nicklaus. I'm gonna make 'em look bad, predict the score, how bad I'm gonna beat 'em, everything – just like I do in boxing. I think I'll quit boxing and start playing golf. I'll get rich – **and besides, that ball can't hit back!"** (October 1974, *Golf Digest*)

And You?

And how about you? Do you find that there is something about golf that is addicting? I surely do. It has this magnetic power to draw us in. We can't help ourselves. Like Ruth, Rice, and Jordan, it's hard for us to stay away from it. Many of us are passionate about it. We love the competition. We love the atmosphere of a golf course. We love the camaraderie that a round of golf provides. We love how relaxing it can be. We love the idea that we can become better at it. And we love how it beckons us back for more.

Golf Term

Cuban

Cuban is a golf term relating to a putt that doesn't quite go in. It is when a putt rolls and rolls and then stops just short of going in the cup. The ball is a Cuban. **It needed one more revolution!**

“Gouff” in the Year 1527

In 1527, Robert Maule made it into the golf history books when he played “gouff” on the Barry Links in Angus, Scotland (near the modern–day town of Carnoustie) as a wager for a drink at a pub. **According to Wikipedia’s *Timeline of Golf History*, his golf outing made him the first–ever commoner on record to play golf.** (Back then a commoner was defined as someone not of noble lineage nor of the priesthood.) Prior to that time, there are accounts of royals participating in the new game, but there was never any mention of a commoner playing it.

Although the details of that round of golf weren’t recorded, let’s think about what it probably was like when Robert Maule played “gouff” in Scotland **nearly 500 years ago.**

The Course

The Barry Links course was a natural one, as were all golf courses at that time. **No one had planned it, designed it, laid it out, or built it.** It was just a stretch of natural grass, bushes, sand, and bunkers situated close to the North Sea on the east coast of Scotland where the wind blew a lot and where the rain was frequent. Nobody mowed anything or tended anything. There were no greens keepers or maintenance people to look after the course. **We're not sure how many holes it had, but it did not have 18.** The game was played over the area's public ground and no fee was charged to play. Most of the greens were double greens, meaning that they were used twice in each round – once while going out away from the town and once more while coming back in.

The Equipment

In 1527, Robert Maule played with the simplest of golf equipment. **He probably only carried one club, a wooden stick that was handmade by either himself or a friend.** The farthest he could hit the stone or the small wooden ball he played with was perhaps 70 or 80 yards. The ball didn't fly or roll very straight and was hard to control. The hole he aimed at on each green had no specific diameter or depth – it was just a large indentation dug out of the ground with the tip of a stick or with the heel of a golfer's shoe. As he teed off on each hole, Robert either hit the ball off the ground or he built up a small mound of dirt or sand and then placed the ball on top of it.

The Clothing

Even when playing golf, Robert and his fellow golfers at that time were rather well dressed, wearing the traditional Scottish clothing we see so often in old Scottish drawings and paintings. Since the course was located by the North Sea, cool, rainy, windy weather was present most of the time. Out on the course, Robert would have dressed in several layers of clothing to help guard against the elements; perhaps **a tweed jacket or patterned wool sweater, a shirt with a starched collar, a necktie, and woolen breeches that ended below the knee.** He probably wore knee socks and sturdy work shoes out on the course. And, of course, a Scotsman wore a hat – probably one that was called a paddy cap made out of tweed, wool, or leather. It was flat on top, slightly rounded at the edges, and had a small stiff brim in front.

The Rules

Few, if any, golf rules existed in 1527, so Robert Maule and his golfing friends were free to make up their own. Competition was **always match play**, not stroke play, meaning that you and your competitor kept track of how many holes each won but not how many cumulative strokes each had. As the game became more popular, regulations and procedures were slowly adopted that eventually became standard rules adhered to by most who played the game.

Robert Maule

And what about Robert Maule? Born in 1497, he was rather tall, well–spoken, and known as a proper gentleman who enjoyed hunting and hawking (using hawks to catch prey). For a period of several years he was the Sheriff of Angus and history records that he once helped defend King James V, the King of Scotland, in a battle. **While doing so, he was captured, carried off to England, and imprisoned for a time in the Tower of London.** In 1560, Robert died at the age of 63 and was buried in Angus at the Panbride Church.

The Barry Burn in 1527 and in Our Day

Oh, and there's something I find quite interesting about that Barry Links layout on which Robert Maule played in 1527. A water hazard called the **Barry Burn** (a burn is a small stream) meandered through the course during Maule's days. Today, the world–renowned Carnoustie Golf Links is located where the Barry Links used to be, **and that same Barry Burn stream still runs through several holes on the course.** You may recall that it was at Carnoustie during the **1999 British Open** that the French golfer **Jean van de Velde** had his infamous meltdown on the 18th hole at Barry Burn. Poised to win the tournament if he could only shoot **a double bogey or better** on that final hole, van de Velde's ball ended up in the Barry Burn and he shot a triple bogey on the hole. In the ensuing three–man playoff, Paul Lawrie won the tournament. Jean van de Velde, **with his trousers rolled up and standing barefoot up to his shins in the water of the Barry Burn,** is still an image I remember vividly from watching that tournament on TV. Do you remember it as well? It all makes me wonder how Robert Maule fared when he encountered the Barry Burn back in 1527. Perhaps it caused him similar trouble.

Some Historical Dates Relating to the Development of Golf

- 1261 – A game known as "colf" (or "kolf") is played in The Netherlands
- **1527 – Commoner Robert Maule plays "gouff" on the**

Barry Links in Scotland

- 1552 – The first recorded reference is made of a game called "golf" being played at St. Andrews
- 1567 – Mary, Queen of Scots, is seen playing golf
- 1618 – The featherie ball is invented in Scotland to replace balls made out of rock and wood
- 1659 – The city of Albany, NY bans golf from its streets – the first reference to golf in America
- 1682 – Andrew Dickson, the first caddie of record, carries the Duke of York's clubs
- 1744 – The first rules of golf are drawn up in Edinburgh, Scotland
- 1764 – Several holes at the Old Course in St. Andrews are combined, reducing the number of holes there from 22 to 18, thereby setting a standard for future courses
- 1848 – The gutta–percha ball is invented by the Reverend Adam Paterson to replace the featherie ball
- 1857 – The earliest mention is made of spikes (initially they were small nails or sprigs) being added to shoes that were worn while golfing to prevent slippage
- 1881 – A dimpled pattern begins to be added to golf balls to improve how they fly through the air
- 1889 – The first golf tee is patented in Scotland by William Bloxsom and Arthur Douglas
- 1933 – Golfers had worn formal British–style clothing for centuries, but a heat wave at the 1933 US Open began to change that. Shirts and pants made of lighter–weight fabrics soon become the accepted style.
- 1939 – The rules of golf are amended to limit players to no more than 14 golf clubs in their bag
- 1988 – The 1.68" diameter golf ball becomes the standard-sized ball worldwide. (The smaller–sized 1.62" ball previously allowed by the R&A is no longer legal.)

(Note – Many of the dates used in this chapter come from Wikipedia's *Timeline of Golf History.)*

Golf Term

Fairway

The word **fairway**, which today we commonly associate with the game of golf, had its origins in the world of ships and seas. **The navigable portion of a harbor or river through which ships entered or left port was known as the fairway.** Likewise, the portion of the golf hole you hope to stay in is called the **fairway.**

(Note – This was first published in the author's book ***Cruising – A View Through the Porthole.***)

Pantone 342

The green jackets worn by the winners of the Masters tournament and by members of the Augusta National Golf Club are a specific and a particular shade of green – Pantone 342. (Pantone is a widely–recognized standardized color matching system.) Although there are dozens of different shades of green in the Pantone system, **it is 342, and only 342, that is used for the jackets.**

Golf, of course, is full of the color green. The next time you are out on the course, just stop for a minute and notice how many different shades of green you see around you. Even the grass on the putting greens shows up in different shades depending on which way the green has been mowed, where the water has been hitting, and what direction the sun is in relation to the green. Those who are experts at reading greens learn about the grain of the grass and how the shade of the green gives hints as to how the putt will break and roll. **And those who have seen Augusta National in person or on TV are amazed by the vibrant, beautiful, and varied green colors of that golf course.**

I wanted to write a chapter for this book about **the green jackets at Augusta National,** so I sent a letter to Billy Payne, the

Chairman of the Augusta National Golf Club in Augusta, Georgia. I asked Mr. Payne if I might have the privilege of visiting his club so that I could obtain information about their green blazers. Ten days later I received a nice letter back from him saying:

> **Dear Mr. Lee:**
>
> **Thank you for your recent letter regarding your new book about golf. Unfortunately, we will not be able to provide the assistance you request for your research on the green jacket. We appreciate your interest and wish you the best on your project.**
>
> **Sincerely,**
> **William Porter Payne**
> **Chairman**

So the following material about Augusta's green jackets has no official verification from Augusta National, but I believe the information is accurate, having gleaned it from a number of other sources over time:

Augusta National's Green Jackets

- The Pantone 342 color for the Masters jackets is often referred to as **brilliant rye green.**
- Since 1967, the jackets have been made exclusively by the **Hamilton Tailoring Company** of Cincinnati, Ohio.
- The material for the jackets comes from the **Victor Forstmann, Inc.** mill in Dublin, Georgia. It is a tropical weight wool and it takes about 2½ to 2¾ yards of cloth to make each jacket.
- Hamilton Tailoring doesn't order the cloth very often, and when they do order it they order about **500 yards at a time.** That's enough to make nearly 200 green jackets.
- The style of the jacket is single–breasted and center–vented and each jacket has brass buttons inscribed with the Augusta National logo. The buttons are made by the **Waterbury Button Company** in Cheshire, Connecticut.
- The Augusta National patch sewn on the left breast pocket is made by the **A&B Emblem Company** in Weaverville, North Carolina.
- The jacket that the winner of the tournament receives at the victory ceremony **is not the one he keeps.** It is merely a member's jacket that the club officials estimate is a close fit for the champion. Later on the winner is properly measured and then the tailors at Hamilton Tailoring are provided the necessary measurements. Once completed, a label with the owner's name is stitched on the inside and the jacket is sent to the winner.
- As a tradition, the winner of the previous year's tournament presents the green jacket to the new champion. This is done on live TV in the famous **Butler Cabin.**
- Except for the winner's jacket, the green jackets that belong to the members of the club and to all past champions **are kept in a cedar closet located on the**

lower floor of the clubhouse. They are only to be worn while at the club and are not to be taken home. The tournament winner, however, is allowed to take his green jacket with him for one year after the victory, and then he has to return it to the club.

- **The original reason for the green jackets at Augusta National had nothing to do with winning the Masters.** Rather, the green jackets were worn by members so that visiting nonmembers could more easily identify club members in case they needed information and help.
- The first Masters champion to be given a green jacket was **Sam Snead in 1949** and as he received that jacket he was made an honorary member of the club. Once that practice began, green jackets were awarded retroactively to all past champions back to when the tournament began in 1934 and all became honorary club members.
- A few of the green jackets have been sold at auction (much to the dismay of the golf club officials who claim that the club owns all of the jackets). In 2013, **Horton Smith's** green jacket was auctioned off for **a little more than $680,000.** Horton Smith was the winner of the very first Masters tournament – and his winning check for that victory was only $1,500!
- The members take **great pride in their green jackets.** Jim James, a past official of the club, was once quoted as saying, "The green jacket is to Augusta National as the Statue of Liberty is to New York or the Mona Lisa is to the Louvre."

Use of Additional Pantone Green Colors

In addition to the Pantone 342 used at Augusta for the jackets, **certain other products and items use specific Pantone green colors.** Here are a few that I found interesting:

- **John Deere tractors** are always painted Pantone 364 green, which is now commonly known as John Deere green. There is even a song called "John Deere Green." Do you perhaps remember it? Joe Diffie came out with it in 1993. It is a love song.

- The green ring in the **Olympic logo** (the 2nd ring from the right) is Pantone 355. Originally, each ring symbolized one of the five inhabited continents of the world, with the green ring representing Australia. Now the five rings are said to symbolize the colors found in the flags of the world.
- Pantone 356 is **Boston Celtic** green.
- **Kermit the Frog** is a Pantone 802 amphibian. His character has been redesigned several times over the years and his shade of green has also changed. Today, Kermit's color is Pantone 802 green, which is often called neon green.
- The green of the **Land Rover** logo is Pantone 795, called bamboo green.
- **US Army green** is Pantone 574 and the color for the **Green Berets** of the US Army Special Forces is Pantone 447, called rifle green.
- The green in the logo on the boxes of **Tic Tac Mints** is Pantone 361. It is known as Tic Tac green.
- And for the green **on the cover of this book,** we used Pantone 354.

Golf Term

Dormie

Mary, Queen of Scots, who was the queen of Scotland from 1542 to 1567, is believed to have been the first woman golfer – and tradition has it that she may also have been the person to contribute the word **dormie** to the game of golf.

From French and Latin, **dormie means to sleep or relax.** (Related words are dormitory and dormant.) In golf it is a word used in match play (like at the Ryder Cup and Presidents Cup) to indicate that one golfer (or team) is leading by the same number of holes as there are holes remaining – such as being 3 holes up with 3 holes to play. **The dormy golfer or golfers can't lose.** They are at the point in the contest where they can relax a bit, knowing that even if their opponent won all of the remaining holes, the match would end in a halve (a tie) at worst.

Now back to Mary. The story goes that one day in Scotland while watching a golf match, Mary, **who was fluent in French,** saw that the golfer who was leading was up by as many holes as were left. She called out that **he was dormie** – meaning that he could just relax and almost sleep through the rest of the match because he couldn't lose.

And the term dormie stuck. We still use it today.

10

"Señor, I Think Your Ball Is in the Jungle!"

Caddies are an interesting part of the game of golf. The word caddie comes from the fifteenth–century French word "cadet," meaning a young man in the army who was an all–around helper and apprentice. First appearing in the English language two centuries later, it came to mean anyone who was hired or employed as a carrier of golf items.

Although I have rarely used a caddie, while vacationing in Puerto Vallarta, Mexico, I played at a beautiful course not far from our hotel. As part of the golf package, a caddie was assigned to each of us in the foursome. **My caddie was a lively 13–year–old boy with dark hair, dark eyes, and a huge smile.** His English was limited, but he made up for it in personality and enthusiasm.

The first and second holes went okay, but my drive on the third hole was a nasty slice that sailed out of sight to the right. The caddie looked at me, shook his head in deep sorrow, and in a heavy Spanish accent said, **"Señor, I think your ball is in the jungle!"** His sad face and his pronunciation of the word jungle with a soft Spanish "j" made our entire group burst out in laughter. Yes, indeed, my errant drive certainly had ended up in the heavy jungle and was nowhere to be found.

Jim "Bones" McKay has been Phil Mickelson's caddie since 1992. As they have teamed together to win five majors and over 40 tournaments, it is estimated that they each have walked over 28,000 miles. And during this entire time Bones has carried Phil's heavy golf bag, a bag that weighs between 35 and 45 pounds. That large leather golf bag typically contains 14 clubs, several golf gloves, about a dozen balls, towels, drinks, snacks, and first–aid items – plus an umbrella and two sets of raingear in case of inclement weather.

Bones is 100% devoted to Phil. In 2008, Bones's younger brother, Tom, got married in Vermont on a Saturday afternoon during a golf tournament that Phil was playing in in Boston. Phil told Bones not to worry about him and golf but to take the week off and go to the wedding. After all, Bones had helped introduce the bride and groom to each other. But Bones adamantly vetoed the idea. **It was inconceivable to him to have Phil play golf without him being on the bag.** Luckily, Phil's Saturday tee time was early in the morning. As soon as the round was over, Bones rented a plane and flew to Vermont, arriving at the wedding ceremony with just minutes to spare. By Sunday he was back in Boston for Mickelson's final round.

Phil loves Bones as a brother. After winning the 2004 Masters, Phil said, "Bones is one of the three most important people in my life. The other two are my wife and my manager. Bones is not just a great caddie, but also a dear friend and trusted confidant."

Caddies on the PGA TOUR are **required to wear clothing prescribed by the host tournament and the PGA TOUR.** They must wear solid–colored Khaki–style long pants which touch the top of the shoe, although tailored knee–length shorts are permitted at some tournaments. A collared shirt must be worn. And shoes must be closed–toe with rubber soles (preferably tennis or basketball shoes). Bright shoe colors that may draw attention to the shoe are not permitted. And additional dress requirements may be in effect at certain tournaments **such as at the Masters.** At that tournament a different uniform must be worn – a uniform consisting of a white Masters jumpsuit, white tennis shoes, and a green Masters cap.

A caddie can earn big bucks if his golfer does well. The compensation that professional caddies receive for their work varies from golfer to golfer. Although there is no standard scale of pay, it is common for a pro's caddie to receive a weekly allowance of $1,000–$1,500 plus a percentage of the golfer's earnings that week. A typical sharing of the winnings might be:

- Golfer makes the cut – caddie is paid 5% of the winnings
- Golfer finishes in the top 10 – 7%
- **Golfer wins the tournament – 10%**

With winning checks reaching as high as $1.8 million at today's big tournaments, there are lucky caddies out there earning $180,000 for their week's work.

The contract that most caddies have with their professional golfer requires that the caddie's conduct be professional and above reproach – both on and off the course – and that he must avoid all illegal and questionable activities. And the last few years, a new clause is showing up more and more in the contracts – the social media clause. A typical one of these clauses might include wording such as: **"The caddie is not to say, write, or place on social media anything that might be derogatory, embarrassing, disparaging, or improper about the golfer or about professional golf."**

As the game of golf grew and progressed over the centuries, the duties of a golf caddie evolved. No longer considered to be just a lowly servant, today's caddie is a very important part of the team. Depending on the wishes, needs, and nature of the professional golfer, the caddie helps set the overall game plan for the tournament as well as the strategy of how to play each individual hole. Besides carrying the bag, giving out yardages, suggesting which club to use, and reading putts, many caddies are looked to by their golfer to give psychological support as well. And in many cases, as with Phil and Bones, they become a valued friend to the golfer, both on and off the course.

Caddies are an interesting part of the game of golf. And although my 13–year–old caddie in Puerto Vallarta never did find my golf ball in the jungle, **with his able assistance and advice, that round of golf turned out to be a most enjoyable experience for me.**

Golf Term

They're Rolling at 7.5

When a golf broadcaster says **"they're rolling at 7.5,"** what does that mean? This number refers to how fast or slow putts are traveling on the greens of the course, **as measured by a Stimpmeter.** The higher the number, the faster the ball is rolling. A measurement of 4.5 or less would be slow, 6.5 is about medium speed, and 8.5 and higher is a fast green. In many sports – golf, bowling, and curling come to mind – the speed of the playing surface greatly affects performance.

Although I'd often heard Stimpmeters mentioned while watching golf tournaments on TV, I had never seen one until I went to our local country club and asked the golf course superintendent to show me one. I expected to see a fairly complicated device with various gauges, moving parts, and battery compartments, **but was surprised to find that a Stimpmeter is about as low tech as you can get.**

It is simply a 36" long by 1¾" wide aluminum bar that has a V–shaped groove running down its entire length. A ball release notch is positioned 6" from one end. To use it, a level area of the green is chosen. The Stimpmeter is laid flat on the green, a golf ball is placed in the notch, and then the end nearest the notch is raised up. When that end is high enough (at about a 20° angle from horizontal), **gravity pulls the ball out of the notch.** On its own power the ball rolls down the length of the bar, across part of the green, and then stops. A tape measure is used to measure how far it has rolled, in feet and inches, from the end of the Stimpmeter. The ball is rolled twice more in the same direction and then three times in the opposite direction. **The six distances are averaged – and that is the Stimpmeter number.** That is the speed of the green.

Designed by golfer Edward Stimpson in 1935, an official Stimpmeter is now a patented item that is only available through the United States Golf Association. They sell for $110, and although they were green in color for many years, the model that is currently available is blue – **a blue called USGA blue.**

De Zwanen Rcgel

(The Swan Rule)

While playing the **Golfclub Old Course Loenen** in The Netherlands, I became aware of an interesting rule of golf for that particular course. It was called **De Zwanen Regel, or the Swan Rule.** Here is a portion of the rule – first in Dutch and then in English:

"Regel bij Zwanen, Zwanennesten, en Zwanenpoep." (Rule Regarding Swans, Swan Nests, and Swan Droppings.)

- "Een zwaan/zwanen, zwanennest(en), en/of zwanenpoep mag als abnormaal terreinomstandigheid worden beschouwd." (Swans, swan nests, and/or swan droppings are to be regarded as abnormal terrain conditions.)
- "Een bal die je niet kan spelen/slaan of oprapen zonder de rust van het dier te verstoren mag zonder strafslag vervangen worden." (If a ball cannot be played/hit or picked up without bothering the animal, the ball may be replaced without a penalty stroke.)

This is an example of what golf calls **a local rule. According to Rule 33–8a of the Rules of Golf, "The Committee may establish Local Rules for local abnormal conditions…"** Typically, local rules deal with such things as the boundaries of the golf course, environmentally sensitive areas, and unusual situations unique to that course (such as the presence of protected swans). Since no two golf courses are the same, local rules are quite common – and they can be quite interesting. For instance:

#1 – The Yellowknife Ravens and Fairways

While playing at the Yellowknife Golf Club in Yellowknife, Canada, which is located about 250 miles south of the Arctic Circle **and is largely built on permafrost,** I discovered some unusual local rules. The fairways have only dirt, rocks, shrubbery, and a few trees – but no grass. And the course is home to many huge, black ravens. So Yellowknife has two particular local rules:

- **Local Rule 24a** – **"There is no penalty when the ball is taken by a raven or any other animal or bird."** (The logo for the course is a raven with a golf ball in its beak.)
- **Local Rule 24b** – **"The ball may be lifted, cleaned, and placed onto a mat."** Before teeing off, the pro at the golf shop gives each golfer a small piece of outdoor carpeting. On each shot out on the course, the player puts down their

piece of carpet, lifts and places the ball on it, and then hits the next shot.

#2 – The Road Hole at the Old Course in St. Andrews

The St. Andrews committee made an interesting local rule for the 17th hole on its Old Course, known as the **Road Hole** because there is an artificially–surfaced road that runs along it. This rule impacted my play on that hole when my drive rolled off the fairway and stopped in the middle of the road. Instead of saying that the golfer may take a free drop if the ball lands on the road, which is the usual rule, they said the opposite. **Their rule says that the road is an integral part of the course and is in play – and that there is no relief (no drop) if the ball ends up on it.** The ball must be hit off of the road – which I did, sculling my second shot and sending it over the green and into the rough.

#3 – Whistling Straits Bunkers

The famous Whistling Straits course near Kohler, Wisconsin is unusual because it has **more than 1,000 bunkers.** Many of these are large, sandy areas that on most courses would be classified as waste bunkers. The Rules of Golf say that a golfer may ground his or her club (i.e. let the club touch the ground during practice swings) in a waste bunker without incurring a penalty, but may not do so in a regular sand bunker. But at Whistling Straits, **the unusual local rule specifically states that all of the 1,000+ sand areas on the course are classified as bunkers,** even if they don't look like a normal bunker. So clubs may not be grounded in them.

Dustin Johnson (and his caddie) forgot about the local rule. On the last hole of the 2010 PGA Championship (the 72nd hole), Johnson's tee shot missed the fairway and landed in an area that looked like a waste area on most other courses. **Johnson grounded his club on his practice swings and was assessed a two–stroke penalty.** The added strokes took him out of a playoff for first place with Bubba Watson and Martin Kaymer. Kaymer ended up winning the two–man playoff and the tournament.

#4 – A Ball Lying in a Bomb Crater

The Richmond Golf Club in Surrey, England **faced a situation during World War II** that required the creation of several unusual local rules. It seemed that bombs were occasionally dropped on or near the golf course during German air raids. Consequently, the following rules were established by the golf club's committee:

- Players are asked to **pick up bomb parts and shrapnel** they may encounter on the course so that mowing machines won't be damaged.
- A player whose stroke is affected by the **simultaneous explosion of a bomb** may play another ball from the same place, if desired.
- **A ball lying in a bomb crater** may be lifted and dropped not nearer the hole. No penalty.

#5 – The Wicker Baskets at Merion

At the Merion Golf Club in Ardmore, PA, **each green has a flag stick with a wicker basket on top instead of a flag.** (This is a carryover tradition from some old courses in Scotland that used sheepherders' wicker baskets instead of flags.) So how is it handled if a golf ball gets stuck in the wicker basket? This is covered by a local rule. This rule says that the flagstick is a movable obstruction. **If the ball happens to get stuck in a wicker basket, the player is granted relief** (that is, the player may move the ball without incurring a penalty). However, in taking relief the player may not place the ball in the hole. **Instead, the player must place the ball on the lip of the hole.**

By the way, the wicker baskets at Merion used to be made by a member of the grounds crew. Now they are made by a woman in South Carolina whose identity is kept secret. Authentic old ones are valuable collector's items. **One was said to have been sold at auction for over $5,500.**

Although I've not yet played at Whistling Straits, Richmond, or Merion, I do have firsthand experience with the swans in

Holland, the permafrost in Canada, and a certain road on a famous golf course in Scotland. How about you? What about the courses you have played on? **Have you noticed any unusual local rules?** And if you have, would you mind sharing them with me? I'd be most interested in hearing about them.

Golf Term

Dominant Eye

Jack Nicklaus is a left–eye–dominant golfer. As you've gone about your life, your brain has built up images of the world you live in using slightly different views from your right eye and your left eye. That's good. As we know, having two eyes helps us see things more clearly and helps us have better depth perception. Over time, our eyes normally grow to become different strengths. **This causes most people to have a dominant eye,** an eye that tends to take priority as we look at things. I have a dominant right eye, as does about 80% of the population.

Studies have shown that your dominant eye can affect your golf game, especially your putting. In putting, golfers who are right–eye–dominant tend to see the hole a bit to the right of its true location. Their putt, therefore, can end up somewhat off course unless they compensate for what their dominant eye is seeing. Quite a few golf instructors teach that to counteract this eye phenomenon, a right–eye–dominant golfer (who golfs right handed) needs to set up for the putt with the ball a little bit back in the stance **so that the right eye is directly over the ball.** This helps the golfer see the line more correctly and hit the ball on line more frequently. A left–eye–dominant golfer who is right handed, like our friend Jack, would want to position the ball more forward in their stance so that the ball is directly under their left eye when preparing to putt. (For left–handed golfers, all of the above adjustments would be just the opposite.)

To determine which is your dominant eye, extend your arms in front of you and make a circle using your index fingers and thumbs. Now look through that circle at an object across the room, such as a clock on the wall. Position the clock in the center of the circle. Now close one of your eyes. **If the clock remains in the center of the circle, the eye that is open is your dominant eye.** However, if the clock appears to be outside of the circle, the eye that you have closed is your dominant eye.

12

10,000 Hours of Deliberate Golf Practice

Dan McLaughlin recently told me that he expects to reach **the 10,000 hour mark** in early 2018 and that he still is on course for reaching his goal.

Starting on April 5, 2010, 30–year–old Dan McLaughlin gave up his employment as a commercial photographer in Portland, Oregon and since then has devoted his time to learning to play golf so that he can make it onto the PGA TOUR as a professional golfer – **by logging 10,000 hours of deliberate golf practice.** His original time schedule was to achieve the 10,000 hours of practice by late 2016.

Why 10,000 hours and what is meant by deliberate golf practice?

In his 2008 book ***Outliers*****, Malcolm Gladwell** put forth the idea that **"ten thousand hours is the magic number of greatness."** His studies had shown that "it is an extraordinarily consistent answer in an incredible number of fields…that you need to have practiced for 10,000 hours before you get good." He said this rule had application in a variety of endeavors, including learning to play musical instruments, mastering chess, and even in excelling in sports. Additional studies in the area of practice and learning by **K. Anders Ericsson,** a Swedish researcher at Florida State University, indicated a strong connection between **extended deliberate practice and excellence in performance** in medicine, music, chess, and sports. (See his book, *The Road to Excellence: The Acquisition of Expert Performances in the Arts and Sciences, Sports and Games.)*

10,000 Hours

By the term "extended deliberate practice" is meant a high concentration of proper practice beyond a person's comfort zone – practice that pushes a person to the limit of their abilities day after day.

Dan McLaughlin decided a few years ago to give it a try. Standing 5'9" and weighing 150 pounds, Dan was not exactly physically gifted for golf, but he was convinced that the research and studies about the 10,000 hours would yield the desired result for him. So, having had no prior experience in golf, he put together a plan **(called *The Dan Plan*)** and with the help of a PGA golf instructor, a strength trainer, a chiropractor, and a goal guru he began to carefully log every single hour along the road to 10,000 hours. **Dan only counts the hours if they are meaningful and deliberate hours.** Just going to the driving range for a while or playing a round of golf without an eye toward error correction and improvement isn't sufficient.

Dan, whom I have not met in person, corresponded with me via email about how he is progressing. Following are his answers to three questions I asked him:

Question: Are you still on course for reaching 10,000 hours in late 2016?

Answer: "No. It has taken me four years to get to the 5,000 hour mark, so my final date for my 10,000th hour will be early 2018 instead of 2016. **I have found that you get fewer high quality focused hours per day than I thought would be possible at the onset.** I am, though, on track handicap wise, although perhaps just a hair back of where I thought I would be at this point." (Since sending this information to me, Dan has sustained a back injury which has slowed him down even more.)

Question: What have you discovered about playing golf that is harder than you thought it would be and what have you discovered that is easier?

Answer: "In general, I would say that **producing a powerful and accurate tee shot consistently is much harder than I had imagined.** The ball is sitting there on the tee in the ground and it seems like it would be easy to hit it out on the fairway, but it is surprisingly difficult. **Putting has been easier than I thought,** as before I began everyone told me that short putts would be knee–knockers and could add to your score easily, but I have found it pretty straight forward to get those into the hole."

Question: Is it still your goal to make the PGA TOUR?

Answer: "Yes! Every day that goal comes a step closer. My ultimate goal is to make it on the PGA TOUR and the harder I work and the more hours I put in, the clearer that path becomes."

Dan's quest is of great interest to me and is something that I plan to continue to follow and to keep an eye on. If you would like to keep track of how he is doing, go to his online blog ***thedanplan.com.*** It is updated regularly and a lot of fun to read.

Personally, I hope Dan makes it. His story would provide an interesting new chapter in the history of learning to play golf. And if Dan pulls it off, then why couldn't we?

Golf Term

Scratch

In my next life I hope to be a scratch golfer – a golfer whose average score for a round of golf is par or better. **A scratch golfer's handicap is zero or below.** Per the USGA, a male scratch golfer is able to hit tee shots an average of 250 yards and can reach a 470–yard hole in two shots – at sea level. Similarly, a female scratch golfer can hit average drives of 210 yards and can reach a 400–yard hole in two shots.

Scratch is a very old Middle English word. In foot races, a shoe or stick was used to draw a starting line in the dirt or sand before the beginning of a race. **This line was the scratch.** To start from scratch meant to begin the race with no advantage or disadvantage – that is, with no head start and with no handicap. In later years in the world of golf, scratch came to mean a golfer with no handicap.

And, as defined by the USGA, **a golfer whose handicap is approximately 18 is called a bogey golfer.** That's not what I want to be in the next life. I've had enough of being that in this life.

Just Add Dimples

The advertisement about **the new ball** caught my eye:

"Our balls are designed with a patented **dimple** design which gives the ball extra stability in the air. Players are able to gain better control of the ball, giving them greater distance and more consistency. The rough surface of the ball creates friction in the air giving the ball greater traction."

And then I saw another ad about **the benefits of dimples**:

"**Dimples** create low–pressure turbulence that reduces drag. Our tests show that these dimples contribute to better overall performance."

A third ad drove home the same point:

"The addition of **dimples** provides for greater aerodynamic flow, translating to higher speeds and improved control."

Well, since this is a book about golf, you'd assume that all three of the above advertisements were about some new and improved golf balls. **But they're not.** The first ad is from **Puma** and talks about their **new soccer ball.** The second ad is promoting

an innovative Nike track uniform. The last ad is from **Zipp**, touting its **new dimpled carbon–composite wheel for racing bicycles.**

Each of these three companies mentions in their ads how their inspiration for adding dimples to their products came from golf balls. Puma says, "The Dimple II CW–System soccer ball design is **similar in nature to a golf ball.**" Nike says, "To understand why we chose to add dimples to our latest track uniform, we first have to understand **why the surface of a golf ball isn't perfectly smooth.**" And Zipp says, "The dimple design for our racing bicycle wheels uses a dimple shape that is **popular in current golf ball design.**"

Golf balls have had dimples for quite a few years. As the story goes, in the mid–1800s, new golf balls were smooth. But as the ball was hit over and over again, the surface of those balls was left with permanent dents. New smooth balls were used for tournaments, but in one match a player ran out of new balls and had to use an old dented one. **As he did so, he and those he played with realized that his old roughed up ball was flying farther and straighter than the smooth one.**

The rest is golf history. Soon golf ball manufacturers were putting patterns and dimples on the golf ball on purpose, with wonderful results.

The key to the performance of golf balls is that when they are hit they have **lots of backspin.** A driver can put as much as 3,000 revolutions per minute on the ball and a wedge can cause up to 10,000 rpm of backspin. Golf balls flying through the air experience two aerodynamic forces – lift and drag. **The dimples on a golf ball increase lift by deforming the airflow around the ball similar to, but not identical to, what happens to the wing of an airplane. They also reduce drag, causing the ball to fly farther than if it were smooth.** In fact, a dimpled golf ball can fly more than twice as far as the same ball without dimples. Contrary to what it might seem, a dimpled ball has only about half the drag of a smooth ball of the same size and weight. And the dimples can also help the ball fly straighter (if the ball is hit correctly) or they can cause the ball to hook and slice (if the ball is hit incorrectly).

By rule, golf balls may not be smaller than 1.68 inches in diameter, but they may be as large as you want. And golf balls may not weigh more than 1.62 ounces, but they may be as light as you want. And how many dimples are allowed? **The number of dimples on a golf ball is not regulated – there is no maximum and no minimum.** But the ball must be completely symmetrical. It must be spherical in shape and have a symmetrical arrangement of dimples on its surface. The dimples do not all have to be the same size, shape, and depth, but **their pattern must be symmetrical.**

So how many dimples are there typically on conforming golf balls? (Conforming golf balls are those that have been tested and approved by the United States Golf Association and the Royal & Ancient Golf Club of St. Andrews. Conforming balls are the only ones allowed in USGA/R&A championships, official competitions, or professional events.) Of the 1,304 conforming golf balls on the latest list of approved balls, **over half of them have between 320 and 350 dimples.** The most common number of dimples is 332. The ball with the least number of dimples on that list has 252 and the one with the highest number has 512.

The drag reduction effect of a dimpled or textured surface has been applied to more than just golf balls. As indicated at the start of this chapter, the dimple technique has been used on soccer balls, track uniforms, and bicycle racing wheels. And there are other applications as well. The surfing industry has experimented with **dimples on the bottom of surfboards,** automobile makers have placed **dimples on some body panels** for racing cars and high–end vehicles, and **certain aerodynamic surfaces on some airplanes are dimpled.**

Surfaces with rough textures that lessen drag and improve control are also found in the animal world. **A good example of this is the shark.** Sharks have a rough skin over their entire body. They are covered with what are called dermal denticles which cause a skin texture that marine biologists find very interesting. These scientists say that the uneven surface of a shark's skin, **similar in effect to the dimples on a golf ball,** helps the shark pass through water more efficiently by reducing drag.

I'm sure that **Greg Norman,** the famous pro golfer nicknamed **The Shark,** would be proud.

Golf Term

Course and Slope Ratings

On the back of most golf score cards (or sometimes on the front) you'll find several numbers that are often misunderstood. They are the course rating and the slope rating numbers. These numbers rate a golf course for the purpose of establishing golf handicaps.

The course rating is a number that predicts the difficulty of a golf course for a scratch golfer (a golfer who shoots par). This number, which is close to the par for the course, is always a number carried to one decimal point – such as 69.8, 71.7, or 73.1. The higher the number, the more difficult the course. Each color of tee on the course has a different course rating.

The **slope rating,** or simply called **the slope**, is a bit more complicated. **The slope rating is a number that predicts the relative difficulty of a golf course for a bogey golfer compared to a scratch golfer.** (A bogey golfer is one whose handicap is approximately 18.) Slope ratings are always a whole number – such as 112, 119, or 132. Each color of tee has its own slope rating and, as with course ratings, the higher the number, the more difficult the course. The word slope as used in slope rating has nothing to do with the slope or slant of the ground on the golf course. **Rather, it refers to the slope of a line on a mathematical graph.**

Course ratings and slope ratings are established by the United

States Golf Association (USGA). Both figures represent the difficulty of a golf course and both enter into the calculation of a golfer's handicap.

14

Midnight Madness Golf

Several years ago, quite by accident, I played in a most unusual golf tournament. **Without realizing the significance of the date, I arrived in Yellowknife, Canada on the morning of June 21, the day of the summer solstice.** Yellowknife sits at 62°26'32" (that is 62 degrees, 26 minutes, 32 seconds) north latitude. That is just 250 miles south of the Arctic Circle. Located on the north shore of the Great Slave Lake, I was in Yellowknife to conduct some business for a couple of days.

As I was walking off the plane and heading towards the luggage area, a nice man began talking to me and asked what brought me to Yellowknife. I explained my purpose in coming and he proceeded to tell me how fortunate I was to arrive on such an important day in the city. Since the summer solstice is the day that has the longest period of daylight in the Northern Hemisphere, Yellowknife marks that day as a day of great celebration in their town – **and a day to hold their midnight golf tournament since the sun doesn't go down that night.** (Technically it goes down a little bit on that day, but it doesn't get dark.) He asked me if I played golf, and when I told him I did, he showed me a flyer posted on the wall of the terminal that explained the tournament. I asked him if they still had available tee times, and he said that he thought they did – but that if they didn't, they certainly would make room for a foreigner who wanted to play.

I rented a car, checked into the Explorer Hotel (the room was noteworthy because it had a double set of blackout curtains), and spent the day conducting business. **Then for dinner I went to the old Wildcat Café down by the float plane pier and had a caribou lasagna dinner.** Not bad food. I then drove over to the Yellowknife Golf Club which is located a bit outside of town. Although mid–evening by then, it was still full daylight when I arrived.

The man at the little pro shop was excited to hear that I wanted to participate in the tournament. He took down my name and home address, gave me a simple set of rental clubs to use (I had my small bag of balls, tees, and a golf glove with me), **and told me that I needed to be back at the course no later than 11:30 p.m. so I could meet my playing partners and get out on the course for the shotgun start right at the stroke of midnight.**

I returned a few minutes before the appointed time and as I was walking up to the pro shop, I heard my name announced over the public address system. "Mr. Van Dam from Utah, will you please come to the golf shop?" At the shop, the golf pro grabbed me by the arm and introduced me to three people who were holding cameras and microphones. **"Mr. Van Dam, these are reporters**

from CTV Canadian Television and they are here to film our tournament. They would like to talk to you." The three proceeded to double–check that I really was from Utah, and then asked if they could put a microphone on me and follow me with their cameras as I played golf. They were intrigued by the fact that someone clear from Utah was in Yellowknife playing in the Midnight Madness Tournament. They explained that they were doing pieces on interesting aspects of golf and that their work would eventually be part of a television golf documentary. They said they would mail me a copy of the program once it had aired.

Well, if you want to be self–conscious and have something ruin your golf game, just let a TV crew mike you and take pictures of your every golf shot. But it was a lot of fun, and they put mikes on my playing partners as well.

As mentioned earlier in the book, the Yellowknife golf course is unique because it is built mostly on permafrost. As a result, very little vegetation grows on it. **The fairways are a combination of dirt, rock, and sand, with just a few straggly pine trees and bushes scattered around. The tees and greens consist of plastic artificial turf.** (They used to be made of oiled sand before being upgraded a few years ago.)

When playing Yellowknife, golfers carry the fairway with them. **Before starting the round, we all were provided with a 6" x 10" portable mat made out of artificial grass.** The course's local rules allowed us to pick up our ball, lay down our piece of plastic grass where the ball had been sitting, and then place the ball on top of it for our next shot. Without this, we would have severely damaged our irons – and we would have hit an even greater number of bad shots than we did.

We finished the tournament just after 4:00 a.m. Although we could see okay the entire time, the light was very flat, making it difficult to gauge distances and to get a feel for how far shots would fly and roll. I'm not trying to make excuses, but none of us shot a very good score, much to the delight of the camera crew. **They wanted something unusual to put in their golf documentary, so they weren't at all unhappy when we skulled shots, missed the ball, and three– and four–putted greens.**

And they especially liked one member of our foursome who turned out to be quite a cut–up and comedian when the cameras were on him.

A few months later CTV sent me a copy of their documentary, which they had titled **"The Ridiculous Obsession."** The 88–minute production included footage from the Midnight Madness Tournament in Yellowknife as well as a number of other interesting and quirky segments about golf. Some of the other ones I especially enjoyed were:

- **Golf Nuts Society of America** – This was a feature about an interesting organization that selects a golf nut of the week and a golf nut of the year. To join the organization, a golfer must take a 60–question quiz **to demonstrate how totally obsessed and whacky they are about golf.** If they score high enough, they are admitted into the society.
- **The Buhl Farm Golf Course** – America's only free public golf venue, the Buhl Farm Golf Course in Sharon, PA is free to anyone who wants to play there. **Funded by a private endowment (The Buhl Farm Trust),** the par 34 nine–hole facility is open from 8:00 a.m. to dusk.
- **The FCA Golf Ministry** – This ministry, sponsored by the Fellowship of Christian Athletes, has as its stated purpose **"to glorify God on the golf course."** They exist "to grow young aspiring golfers into biblically mature leaders who transform culture." Their headquarters is in Ponte Vedra Beach, FL.
- **The Moon Course** – Wanting to get a jump on the future, a group of golfers has put together an organization that says they own golf club property for a course that doesn't yet exist. The course's location is on the moon. **As a group, they have a deed for a section of land on the moon on which they hope to develop a course – once the time is right.**

My stay in Yellowknife was well spent, both from a business

aspect and from a golf standpoint. I still can't believe how fortunate I was to be there at the summer solstice. And I'm glad I had my little bag of balls and other golf items with me **because you never know what interesting, exciting, and unusual adventures might present themselves to you on a trip.**

Golf Term

Links

The word **links** associated with the game of golf does not have any connection to the word **links** associated with links of sausage. They have different origins. The one referring to sausage comes from the word **lænks,** which is an old Danish/German term **meaning a chain or a joint.** The word links used in golf has its origin in Scotland where **hlinc** was **an area of rolling ground near the sea, usually consisting of sand dunes and grass.**

In golf, a links course is a specific type of golf course – one that is characterized by rolling fairways, rough grass, few if any trees, and natural sand bunkers. The Royal Troon, Turnberry, and Carnoustie courses in Scotland are true links courses.

Links can also mean **the entire game of golf** – as in, **"Let's go hit the links this afternoon."**

Are Golfers Athletes?

Are golfers athletes? When you see a seriously overweight person wearing plaid shorts standing on a tee box holding a golf club in one hand and a cell phone in the other, it's a little hard sometimes to say that golfers are athletes. But I think for the most part they are. **Per the dictionary, an athlete is a person who is trained in or good at sports, games, or exercises that require physical skill, agility, and strength.** Golf certainly requires a degree of skill, agility, and strength and most golfers are somewhat or quite a bit trained in it. And I don't see anything in the definition of an athlete that says you have to excel at your sport. You just have to be able to participate in it.

Think of the Olympic Games and the hundreds of athletes – **for the International Olympic Committee calls all Olympic participants athletes** – who march in during the opening ceremony and then compete in the games. Most are highly skilled and have very athletic bodies, but isn't it interesting to watch some of the others who are proud to be there to compete for their particular country even though they may not be very good at their sport and don't appear to be athletic? **Remember Eddie "The Eagle" Edwards** who was the first person to represent Great

Britain in Olympic ski-jumping? **He was terrible.** But he was an Olympic athlete. A decided underdog, he finished dead last in both the 70–meter and the 90–meter events – yet we all fell in love with him and rooted for him. (And we should note that golf is now back in the Olympics after a 112–year hiatus. It was dropped from the games after 1904 and was finally brought back for the 2016 Olympics in Rio.)

Not long ago I listened to a lively discussion on a national sports call–in show about whether or not golfers are athletes. No particular conclusion was ever reached, but a lot of interesting points were brought out on both sides. **So what do you think? Are golfers athletes?**

A few years ago, ESPN.com did a really interesting study. They took 60 sports and measured them up, down, inside, and out, and then ranked them according to **which were the toughest to compete in – i.e. which were the most demanding.** A panel of eight experts including several sports scientists, some sports journalists, and a two–sport star athlete identified 10 categories or skills that go into athleticism. These categories were:

- Strength
- Endurance
- Power
- Speed
- Hand–eye coordination
- Flexibility
- Durability
- Analytic aptitude
- Nerve
- Agility

The panel then gave each sport a score in each category on a scale of one to ten. They added up the scores, averaged them, and created a ranking.

Do you want to take a stab at where golf ended up on the list and which sport they placed as number one? Their measurements indicated the following:

The Most Demanding Sports
- **#1 – Boxing**
- **#2 – Ice Hockey**
- **#3 – Football**

The Least Demanding Sports
- **#58 – Shooting**
- **#59 – Billiards**
- **#60 – Fishing**

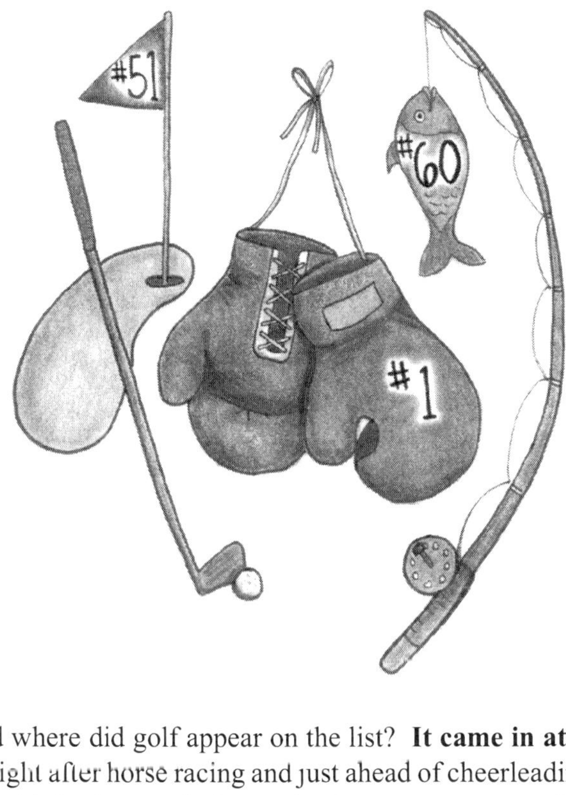

And where did golf appear on the list? **It came in at #51 out of 60,** right after horse racing and just ahead of cheerleading. Golf scored high in analytic aptitude, power, and hand–eye coordination. It scored low in speed, agility, and durability.

Golf, even at the lowest levels, requires some skill and some athletic ability – and even though it doesn't involve running, jumping, or contact it still can be quite rigorous and demanding. And we have learned in the last few decades that golf at the highest levels requires more athleticism than it used to. Most of today's leading pro golfers are strong, powerful, agile, smart, and very fit. They work out a lot and take their conditioning seriously.

Golf is viewed differently by different people. To some, it is exciting to play and wonderful to watch. To others, they find it slow and rather boring. Pat Summerall, the Hall of Fame play–by–play sportscaster was once praised for his ability to call any sport on television – **even golf.** With tongue in cheek he responded, **"Oh, calling golf is easy, 'cause nothing happens."** Personally, I love both playing and watching golf. And I do feel that golfers are athletes – but I know that this is being generous to some of them.

Now that we've settled, at least in my mind, the big question about golfers being athletes, **there remain additional deep and highly important sports questions to be discussed and debated** – especially if you are a sports nut. Questions such as:

- Is golf even a sport or is it more correctly called a game or a recreational activity?
- Are NASCAR drivers, ballroom dancers, horse shoe pitchers, competitive hot dog eaters, and skydivers athletes?
- Who is the best basketball player ever, MJ or someone else?
- Should the diameter of the golf hole be increased?
- What is the greatest individual record in sports?
- Who is the biggest draft bust ever?
- Should players who have used performance enhancing drugs be allowed into their particular sport's hall of fame?
- What is the greatest sports movie of all time?
- Are professional athletes overpaid?

Let the never–ending sports debates continue.

Golf Terms

Sand Trap or Bunker?

In a Peanuts cartoon, a dismayed Snoopy is shown standing in a bunker with a wedge in his hand as he is getting ready to hit his golf ball that is imbedded in the sand. The caption says:

"Mondays are the sand traps in the fairway of life!"

The terms **sand trap** and **bunker** are often used interchangeably as we play golf. **Technically, however, bunker is the correct term.** The word bunker is an old English term that refers to an indentation or shelf. When applied to golf, it is a depression on a course (it can be natural or man–made) that may be filled with sand, long grass, dirt, pine straw, or other things.

The term bunker is a word found in the official Rules of Golf. The term sand trap is not an official golf term. **The rules only talk about bunkers.** Sand trap is a vernacular term – a common term – used by many golfers when they talk about a bunker that has sand in it.

And some advice to those who greet golfers after their round.

"If a golfer comes home with sand in his pant cuffs, don't ask him what score he shot."

16

Psst… Wanna Buy Some Golf Clubs?

Shopping in Hong Kong is a lot of fun. When we lived there, we often went to Mong Kok (located on the Kowloon Peninsula) to check out the amazing bargains found there. **Mong Kok, which means busy corner in Chinese, is described by Guinness as the most densely–populated place in the world – 340,000 people per square mile,** and that doesn't include the thousands of visitors and tourists who flock there daily. It is a jam–packed place where you can shop for nearly everything you can think of. In fact, entire streets in the Mong Kok area are devoted to a single type of product, such as:

- **Ladies Street (Tung Choi Street)** – an amazing number of shops and booths specializing in women's clothing, jewelry, purses, shoes, cosmetics, and a variety of other items
- **Sneakers Street (Fa Yuen Street)** – a host of small retail shops selling running shoes, sports equipment, and sports clothing

- **Bird Street (Yuen Po Street)** – a long line of shops with birds, bird cages, and pet supplies
- **Flower Market Road (Prince Edward Road)** – this street and the nearby side streets are packed with vendors and florist shops selling flowers and plants
- **Electronics Street (Sai Yeung Choi Street)** – dozens of shops selling consumer electronic products, computers, phones, watches, cameras, and music
- **Goldfish Street (Tung Choi Street)** – an entire street of hawkers and shops selling tropical freshwater fish, marine fish, and aquarium accessories
- **Kitchenware Street (Shanghai Street)** – a slew of stores selling products for home and commercial kitchens
- **Tile Street (Portland Street)** – more than 50 stores selling tile, countertops, wall paper, bath tubs, toilets, and sinks

Even though much of the merchandise in Mong Kok is legitimate, **it is also a haven for knock–offs and fake brand–name products.** So when I decided to buy a new set of golf clubs, I avoided Mong Kok and its bargains and instead went to the Star Ferry area of Kowloon where a number of golf shops are located. I wanted to make sure my clubs were not knock–offs, so I only went to shops displaying the Hong Kong Tourism Board's Quality Tourism Services seal and which also indicated that they were authorized dealers for the top brands of golf equipment. To confirm these claims, I visited the Hong Kong Tourism Board's web site and also the web sites of golf manufacturers such as Titleist, Callaway, and TaylorMade. **Quite quickly I was able to verify the authenticity and honesty of several golf shops located in that area.** Then I began the enjoyable process of looking at golf equipment and seeing what kind of a deal I could come up with – because I love bargaining in Hong Kong.

I took extra precautions when buying the clubs because of the horror stories I had heard about fake golf equipment. One such story involved a friend of mine who purchased a brand–name set of clubs in a foreign country he was visiting. The first time he used them, he noticed that the sound that the driver made when it hit the ball was kind of different. Before the end of his first round, the head of the club had worked its way loose and had fallen off. Although he had saved several hundred dollars, **the clubs were knock–offs and his purchase was a waste of good money.**

Some of the problems commonly associated with knock–off golf equipment and what might happen when you play with them are:

- **Problem** – Cheap and inferior adhesives are used to connect the various parts
- **Result** – Heads fall off, heads twist on the shafts, grips come loose

- **Problem** – Heads are not manufactured properly, causing the sizes and lofts of the heads to be off
- **Result** – Clubs are inconsistent, balls come off the club

head at wrong angles, accuracy is decreased, shots are erratic, the clubs in a set of irons are improperly matched with each other

- **Problem** – Use of inferior or substitute materials
- **Result** – Distance is compromised, driver heads don't perform as designed, sweet spots are not per spec, solid hits are less frequent, grips don't feel right and deteriorate rapidly, shafts bend, warp, or shatter

- **Problem** – Graphics are cheap and incomplete
- **Result** – Colors are bland and not per spec, labels are not attached properly, graphics fade and are hard to read, words are spelled incorrectly

The U.S. Golf Manufacturers Anti–Counterfeiting Working Group says:

> **"It is estimated that as many as 2 million counterfeit golf clubs are produced each year.** To put that number in perspective, if you laid every fake club end–to–end they would stretch from Bethpage Black (in New York) to Pebble Beach (in California) and back again. And that doesn't even take into account the millions of fake balls, bags, gloves, and apparel produced."

The organization then goes on to say that up to 95% of fake golf clubs are sold through internet sites. Several of the major golf manufacturers have warnings on their web sites about fake golf products. For example, here is the warning from Callaway Golf:

> **"Counterfeit Club Warning.** To protect our valued customers from fraud, Callaway Golf shares the following warning: Consumers all around the world have been duped into purchasing so–called 'brand new, authentic Callaway Golf products' at very low prices on eBay.com and other internet auction and online retail sites that have turned out to actually be low–quality fakes. Sales of counterfeit Callaway Golf products on such sites have dramatically increased over

the last few years."

So here are a few thoughts to consider when purchasing golf equipment in order to help steer clear of knock–offs:

- Only buy golf equipment from authorized dealers.
- If the price seems too good to be true, it probably is too good to be true. Don't make the purchase.
- Does the seller say the price for the brand–new equipment is at a low bargain–basement level because "the clubs were a gift I didn't need" or "I won the clubs in a tournament or raffle?" If so, be extremely cautious. Sellers often use these types of stories to con their victims.
- If you are in doubt about a potential purchase, call or email the purported manufacturer of the golf equipment before committing to the transaction. They will be glad to help you know if the clubs are theirs and if they are authentic.
- Be extra cautious when purchasing golf equipment on the internet. Even reputable sites may unknowingly be selling counterfeit items.
- Be careful about sending money to people you don't know. This is especially true when buying golf equipment from an overseas source. If the equipment you have purchased is counterfeit, it may be confiscated by U.S. Customs as it arrives in our country, and if so, you'll never even see the equipment – and good luck in trying to get your money back.
- Take the time to carefully study the seller's photos of the equipment you are planning to purchase. Ask for close–ups. Look at the smallest details. Then compare those photos with the identical piece of equipment available at an authorized dealer. Most brand–name golf manufacturers do not sell clubs that are seconds or have blemishes, so if you see any discrepancies, even small ones, the equipment you are planning to purchase may be counterfeit.
- If you do end up with counterfeit equipment, do two

things immediately. First, report the problem to the online web site where you purchased the product (if it was an online purchase), and second, report what happened to the manufacturer whose name appears on the clubs.

It has now been several years and I am still enjoying the set of clubs I purchased in Hong Kong. **They are excellent and have really helped my golf game.** I am happy that I was able to bargain a bit and save a little money on them when I made the purchase. And it makes me feel really good to know that my money didn't make it into the pockets of some dishonest merchants who make their living selling knock–off name–brand golf equipment.

Golf Term

Cross–Dominance

Cross–dominance is a motor skill phenomenon where a person uses one hand for most tasks but prefers the other hand for others. A common example of cross–dominance is a person who uses one hand to write and the other to play sports. **Phil Mickelson and Mike Weir, who are naturally right–handed, are cross–dominant golfers. They both play the sport left–handed.** Cross–dominance often manifests itself in the world of sports, especially with people who are naturally left–handed. Because left–handed golf clubs or a baseball glove for a left–hander weren't available when the person was first learning the sport, they developed an expertise with their off hand and usually stuck with that even after the right equipment became available to them.

Phil Mickelson and Mike Weir, however, are a different story. Phil plays golf left–handed because **he learned how to play golf by mirroring his father's right–handed golf swing.** It worked so well for him that he has always used left–handed golf clubs. **Mike's use of left–handed clubs goes back to the fact that he is a Canadian whose first sport as he was growing up was ice hockey.** As with many Canadian hockey players who are right–handed, Mike began playing with a left–handed hockey stick because it felt more natural to him to hit slap shots left–handed. When he realized he wouldn't grow large enough to be a great hockey player, he picked up golf instead and used left–

handed clubs because they felt better to him.

We even have a cross–dominant golfer in our own family. **My brother–in–law, Reid, who is an excellent golfer, plays golf right–handed even though he is naturally left–handed.** Reid says that right–handed clubs just felt better to him than left–handed ones. It wasn't because left–handed clubs weren't around when he was picking up golf as a young boy, it was because right–handed ones were more natural for him.

And me? I'm a 100% right–handed person and golfer. I can't do a thing with my left hand.

Just a note about a well–known variation of cross–dominance – ambidexterity. When a person is equally adept at using either hand, they are called **ambidextrous.** They are neither right–handed nor left–handed. They are both–handed.

17

Grandpa's Golf Gizmo

Grandpa's Golf Gizmo is a game we invented and built over a period of several years that is located in the far corner of our back yard. We had already built a two–story clubhouse there for our children when they were young, and as they grew up and had their own kids, we thought it would be fun if we added something to it – such as a contraption using golf balls – to create some added activities for the grandchildren. We gave it a name and a logo – **Grandpa's Golf Gizmo** – and invited our family members and friends to come use it. **The final product, which is attached to the clubhouse, fences, and trees in that area of the yard, weaves in and out, up and down, and runs all over the place.** The golf balls are of six different colors and each ball is imprinted with the logo shown on the next page. Although the Gizmo can make quite a racket when all 24–dozen colored golf balls are in motion at the same time, our neighbors so far have been kind and have not complained too much.

Grandpa's Golf Gizmo consists of wooden ramps, pulleys, winches, buckets, a horn, a wooden spoon catapult, 288 golf balls, a pinball machine launcher, a swing, colored name plaques, a draw bridge, stoppers, an escape ladder, a trap door, tubes, ropes, a flag with the logo, colored dice, a board with dozens of bolts sticking out for a game we call Glinko, a cow bell, score cards, a secret compartment, a golf net, chimes, and a golf ball retriever. Over the years our grandchildren, as well as many others, have played with it for countless hours.

Grandpa's
Golf Gizmo

For this chapter of the book, I asked each of our seven grandchildren to draw pictures and to tell me their thoughts about **Grandpa's Golf Gizmo.** The following pages show what they came up with:

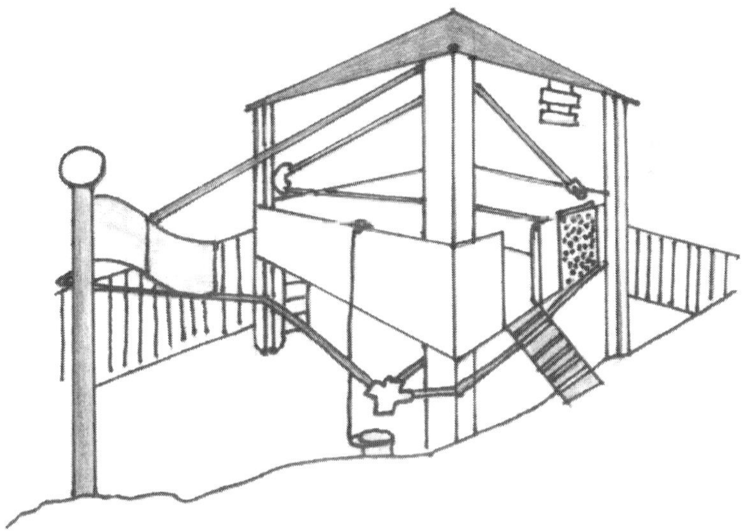

Adam – “I like all the ramps and stoppers and have had lots of fun playing with Grandpa’s Golf Gizmo. It’s like a life–sized pinball machine. It sure beats playing video games!”

Matthew – "I really like the wooden spoon that is a catapult, although it's kind of hard getting the balls to land on the ramp. And I especially like playing Glinko because you can never tell which spot the ball is going to end up in."

Sophie – "Grandpa, I like how there's so much stuff to play with and that you're never bored. And I love seeing my name plaque hanging up when I come. It makes me feel special."

Ben – "I like the really cool draw bridge and trap door and that it's not just a normal door. It's fun to use. And I like trying to shoot the balls up with the pinball machine launcher because it's tricky."

Emmie – "Even after I've played with it for a long time, I don't want to go home. I wish I could stay forever. And I like the secret hiding compartment – but I can't tell you where it is because it's a secret – and then it wouldn't be a secret anymore."

Macie – “When I play at Grandpa’s with Sophie and Emmie, we usually line up all of the rainbow colored balls behind the stoppers and then let them go all at once. I love the sound they make. And I like the bucket on the rope so you can lift all the balls back up into the clubhouse without having to go down to get them.”

Andrew – "Almost every time I come, Grandpa has added a new thing to it. I never run out of stuff to try. And I like putting up the yellow Grandpa's Golf Gizmo flag that Grandma made."

Golf Term

On the Clock

Many sports are all about time clocks and time. I like that golf is different – that we can engage in it **without worrying too much about the clock** – except in three instances:

Being Put on the Clock

The Rules of Golf state that "the player must play without undue delay." (Rule 6–7) In tournaments, if a golf group is slow and has fallen behind, they may be put **on the clock** by golf officials. This typically happens when they are at least one hole or more behind the group in front of them and they are obviously playing very slowly. Once they are **on the clock**, each golfer is timed and if they don't play their shots without undue delay, **they may receive a warning, a penalty, or even disqualification.**

Lost Ball

When looking for a lost ball, **a player is penalized if he searches for it for more than the five minutes** permitted under Rule 27–1.

Ball on the Lip of the Cup

Have you ever hit a putt that ends up hanging over the lip of the cup? Rule 16–2 says that if this happens to you, you are given reasonable time to reach the hole **plus 10 seconds** to wait for the putt to drop. If the ball doesn't fall in the cup within that amount of time, it is considered to be at rest and you have to tap it in. Waiting longer than 10 seconds can result in a penalty.

18

Practice Makes Permanent

Is golf really that difficult to master? Is a golf ball really that hard to hit? You certainly would think so in light of the dozens, if not hundreds, of training aids and practice products available to golfers. And for football? As I visited our largest local sporting goods retailer, I counted that they had four football training aids out on their shelves. For tennis they had just two. And six for soccer. But golf? By my count, **this sporting goods retailer had 64 golf training aids and practice products on display** – and on their web site they had dozens more. And several other on–line sports merchandisers I checked on had even more than that.

Every year in January, a huge golf exhibition is held in Orlando, Florida called the **PGA Merchandise Show.** Nearly ten miles of aisles crisscross over 1 million square feet of space to show off merchandise from more than 1,000 companies. **Over 40,000 attendees come from all 50 states and more than 75 foreign countries to see the latest technology in golf and to look at new and innovative golf equipment, apparel, accessories, and services.** The show looks like it would be a lot of fun to attend, but I've never gone because it is a trade–only show. It's not open to the public. I'm not invited. A person must be a PGA professional, a golf retailer, a member of the media, or an industry leader in order to be granted admittance. They tell me, though, that once I publish this book about golf, I will be able to attend the show and receive a "non–editorial media badge (non–reporting)," whatever that is. Sounds fun. I hope to take them up on the invitation.

The PGA Merchandise Show started small about 50 or 60 years ago when several golf merchandisers got together at a golf club in Florida to show off their golf stuff. At that time, just a corner of a parking lot was sufficient space for them. Eventually it grew to where a tent was needed to accommodate the growing amount of merchandise and people. By 1975 it had moved indoors and then by the 1990s it had grown into one of the largest sporting shows in the world. Now there are golf merchandise shows in many places around the globe **with the one in Orlando being the biggest.**

A review of the list of exhibitors and products at the PGA Merchandise Show indicates that, after golf equipment and golf apparel, **golf training aids and practice products make up the next largest segment.** These items can be grouped into several general categories:

- Putting aids
- Swing aids
- Short game aids
- Books and DVDs
- Aids to improve strength
- Nets, mats, balls, and targets

I'm sure that I could personally benefit from using products in each of these areas as I continue my eternal quest to improve my golf game. As to which specific items would help me the best and would be the most cost–effective, I'm not sure, but I have narrowed it down to **ten training aids and practice products** I have noticed in stores, seen advertised on TV, or have read about in books and magazines that look quite interesting to me. (I have picked out a specific product and a specific manufacturer for each item. Please note that similar devices are often available from other manufacturers.)

- **Orange Whip Trainer,** by Orange Whip, $109.99 – This training aid consists of a black flexible shaft with a heavy grip on one end and a weighted orange ball on the other. The manufacturer claims that practicing with this club will improve the rhythm, balance, tempo, and timing of your swing. This presently is one of the hottest training aids among both pros and amateurs.
- **Tour Sticks,** by Tour Sticks Golf, $14.99 – This is a set of two smooth fiberglass rods that help golfers with their alignment. The instructional booklet that comes with the sticks shows how they can be used for full swing drills, putting drills, short game drills, and set–up drills. Although just two straight sticks, they provide a world of information to the user about their swing and are popular among many top golf instructors and golfers of all abilities. (Note: Kellie Stenzel, a top PGA teaching professional, said, "I think you should always practice with an alignment aid.")
- **Ball–First Trainer,** by SKLZ, $19.99 – Many golfers try

to sweep the ball off the grass with their irons rather than hitting the ball first and then the ground. This simple, J–shaped mat helps train you to impact the ball first. The manufacturer says, "It encourages a proper lag, a downward strike, and a square club at impact." (Note – Gary McCord in his book *Golf for Dummies* says, "The only time you should lift something is when you rearrange your living room furniture. Never try to lift a golf ball with your club. You should hit down with every club except the driver and the putter.")

- **Ben Hogan's Five Lessons,** by Ben Hogan, $17.00 – Ben Hogan was one of golf's greatest ball strikers. He set the standard for how to hit a golf ball. This classic book, published in 1957 and still popular today, is considered to be one of the best golf instructional books ever.
- **Smash Bag Impact Trainer,** by SKLZ, $24.99 – Designed to help teach "the moment of truth" – i.e., the feeling of the correct impact when the club hits the golf ball – the Smash Bag is a heavy–duty bag that you fill with towels, blankets, or clothes. You then swing away at it and watch where you hit the bag and listen to the sound your club makes. "Smash Bag helps eliminate fat and thin golf shots, helps cure slices, and improves overall accuracy," according to the manufacturer. This concept of hitting a heavy bag with your club in order to improve your game has become very popular, especially with beginning to intermediate golfers.
- **Putting Alignment Mirror,** by EyeLine Golf, $39.95 – The manufacturer says that poor alignment is the major cause for missed putts and that this device is perfect for checking all parts of your putting alignment and setup. The idea is very simple – and this product is considered to be very effective at improving your setup and alignment while putting.
- **Medicus Dual Hinge Driver,** by Medicus, $159.95 – A fun training aid to use, this club has a sticky dual hinge located about a third of the way up the shaft. The hinge

is engineered to break or collapse when the club is swung off tempo, out of balance, or off plane, thus giving you instant feedback when you are not swinging correctly. The Medicus driver comes with an instruction manual and DVD. It has been around for quite a few years and has the distinction of being the best–selling golf training aid of all time.

- **The Perfect Impact System,** by LH Golf LLC, $67.00 – Consisting of over 2½–hours of instruction, this is considered by many to be the most comprehensive golf instructional video out. Individual segments include, "Permanent Fixes for Common Faults," "Practice that Actually Lowers Your Score," and "7 Days to Longer Drives." The training is only provided in a digital format and is not available on DVD.
- **Swing Accelerator,** by SKLZ, $99.99 – This is a full–sized driver with a heavily weighted head "to help ingrain the feel of the correct swing path and to improve ball impact," according to the manufacturer. "It increases the strength and flexibility of golf–specific muscles." (Note – Lee Trevino once said that the best training aid he ever used was a simple weighted club.)
- **Golf Ball Finder Glasses,** by PGA TOUR, $24.99 – These specially tinted glasses come with two interchangeable lenses – one blue and one grey. PGA TOUR claims the blue lens helps filter out foliage and grass so that white golf balls stand out. Although more of a golf gadget than a training aid, these eyeglasses look pretty cool when worn – and if they perform as advertised how can you pass them up?

Vince Lombardi, the famous NFL coach, said, "Practice doesn't make perfect. Perfect practice makes perfect." Someone else said, **"Practice makes permanent."** These quotes certainly apply to the use of golf training aids and practice products. Accompanied with good instruction, these items can help us achieve solid golf fundamentals. David Leadbetter, one of the world's top golf instructors, likes training aids. He said, "Teaching aids are the most effective way to build a repeatable swing." Hopefully the right use of golf training aids and practice products can assist all of us in learning to hit a greater number of successful golf shots out on the course – **because hitting a golf ball correctly really is difficult to master.**

Golf Term

Foozle

To foozle means to do slipshod work – and when applied to golf it means to hit a really bad shot. From old German, **fusel meant to do something in a clumsy manner.** Once a very common golf term, it is now making a comeback among many of today's players. Personally, I like the word foozle because it kind of sounds like what it means. **I certainly have foozled my share of golf shots.**

One of the earlier quotes from golf that included the word foozle was when British Prime Minister Arthur Balfour (Prime Minister from 1902 to 1905) said, "There is always hope that a bad drive may be redeemed by a fine approach shot, **or that a foozle with the brassy** may be balanced by some brilliant performance with the iron." And in 1969, Jack Nicklaus made good use of the word when, after finishing a mediocre round, he said to a reporter, "I had a 75, which featured **a couple of foozled short putts."**

19

How's Your Local Muni Doing?

Not long ago I had a chat with the head pro of a municipal golf course in our area. Poor guy. He's frustrated and feeling pretty low. **He needed something to boost his morale, so I made a point of telling him how much I appreciated him and his fine golf course.** He works really hard and does a great job, but despite his efforts, the city is considering closing his course – at least that is what will happen if the citizens in a city–wide election choose to "repurpose" his course. In this instance, "repurposing" means that the city will close down the golf course and make the area into a multifaceted regional park.

A recent Salt Lake City newspaper article by Katie McKellar about the city's golf situation says, "The city has reported its golf program has **more than an $800,000 operating deficit** and needs **more than $20 million in upgrades** over the next 10 to 15 years." This Deseret News article goes on to say, "Analysis of the city's golf fund has indicated an overall decline in play at Salt Lake City golf courses of **18 percent** since 2001." Nationally, similar scenarios are taking place with many municipal courses (as well as public courses) facing financial challenges and possible closure. On average, over 100 courses in our country have closed their doors **each year** during the last several years due to the overbuilding of new courses coupled with a decline in golf participation.

Golf courses come in three basic types: **municipal, public, and private.**

Municipal golf courses (often referred to as munies) are owned by a governmental authority – a city, town, county, or even a state. They exist for the benefit of residents of the municipality, as well as for visitors. Although many municipal golf courses make money, they typically do not have profit as their primary motive. Rather, their purpose is to provide outdoor recreation for local residents. Even though some have excellent facilities, municipal courses often are simple operations with only a basic pro shop, a lunch counter, and a limited selection of clubs and clothing in their golf shop. When a muni has a negative cash flow, the government body that owns it has to subsidize it – from taxes and/or from long–term bonding. And when the citizens of that municipality don't want to subsidize it any more, it often gets closed down.

Public golf courses are privately owned, but the course is open to anyone. Their purpose is to make money for their owners. Many public courses are associated with real estate developments or luxury resorts. They often have very nice facilities such as large club houses, full–service restaurants, extensive golf shops, upscale locker rooms, etc.

Private courses are owned by a golf club or private entity on behalf of its members – usually on a nonprofit basis. Membership is exclusive. An example of this type of golf course is your local country club. Typically, only members and their guests are allowed to play. Memberships and golf fees are normally quite expensive at private courses. Only about 20% of all golf rounds are played on private courses.

Let's look at ten well–known golf courses around the world, all of which are very successful financially. Can you correctly identify which ones are municipal, which are public, and which are private?

1. **Torrey Pines,** La Jolla, California
2. **Augusta National Golf Club,** Augusta, Georgia
3. **The Old Course,** St. Andrews, Scotland
4. **Chambers Bay,** University Place, Washington
5. **Pebble Beach,** Pebble Beach, California
6. **The TPC Sawgrass Stadium Course,** Ponte Vedra, Florida
7. **Whistling Straits,** Kohler, Wisconsin
8. **Shadow Creek Golf Course,** Las Vegas, Nevada
9. **Bethpage Black,** Long Island, New York
10. **Pine Valley Golf Club,** Clementon, New Jersey

Here are the answers:

1. **Torrey Pines** is owned by the city of San Diego. It is a **municipal** course with 36 golf holes. Torrey Pines has hosted the U.S. Open and is scheduled to do so again. In order to make the popular weekend tee–times equally

available to all, golfers are allowed to begin lining up at 6:00 p.m. the night before for tee times starting at 7:30 a.m. the following day. Torrey Pines is one of the finest municipal courses anywhere.

2. **Augusta National** is a **private** course – very private. Its membership is largely kept confidential and until recently it only allowed males to be members. But in 2012, Condoleezza Rice (former U.S. Secretary of State), Darla Moore (a highly successful businesswoman), and Ginni Rometty (CEO of IBM) were invited to join. Augusta National hosts the Masters, the only major that takes place at the same course each year.
3. **The Old Course in St. Andrews** is a **municipal** course owned by the city of St. Andrews. (Technically, it is held in trust by The St. Andrews Links Trust under an act of Parliament.) It is one of the oldest courses in the world and is hugely popular.
4. **Chambers Bay** is a **municipal** course owned by Washington State's Pierce County. It is a very difficult links–style course that came into prominence in 2015 when it hosted the U.S. Open. Because of the idiosyncrasies of its design and layout, it created a great deal of discussion and some controversy during the Open.
5. **Pebble Beach** is a **public** golf course. Although all have access to the course, only resort guests (those staying in Pebble Beach Company lodging) may reserve a tee time more than 24 hours in advance. Pebble Beach has been sold several times, most recently to a group of investors including Clint Eastwood, Arnold Palmer, and Peter Ueberroth. The selling price? Over $800 million.
6. **The TPC Sawgrass Stadium Course's** signature hole is the 17th hole, a short par three known simply as the island green. That hole is world famous. It is estimated that over 100,000 golf balls are retrieved from the lake surrounding the hole each year. In one pro tournament, more than 50 balls were hit into the water around the green in just one round. It is a **public** course owned by the PGA TOUR.

7. **Whistling Straits** is a **public** course owned by the Kohler Company. It has hosted PGA Championships as well as a Ryder Cup. A herd of Scottish blackface sheep call Whistling Straits their home. They are allowed to wander the course freely during the golf season. Whistling Straits is a walking–only course.
8. **The Shadow Creek Golf Course** in Las Vegas is touted as perhaps the most expensive **public** golf course in America with green fees as high as $500, which includes a round trip limo ride from your hotel to the course. In order to play there, a golfer must be a guest at an MGM resort. Former President George H. W. Bush has been a regular at Shadow Creek. Besides playing golf there, rumor has it that he keeps a fishing pole above his locker so he can fish the ponds and brooks on the course. And apparently Shadow Creek has never been shown on TV.
9. **Bethpage Black** is a **municipal** course owned by the state of New York. It is part of Bethpage State Park. In 2002 it became the first publicly owned and operated course to host the U.S. Open. Reservations for the Black Course are limited to one reservation per person per month. But for the first hour of tee times each day, six walk–up foursomes are allowed to play. Bethpage Black is famous for its waiting lines for those early tee times.
10. **Pine Valley** is rated by many golf experts as one of the finest golf courses in the world (out of some 34,000 courses world–wide). It is a very exclusive **private** course with male–only membership. Women guests are permitted to play the course only on Sunday afternoons. Its design is especially noteworthy. The architect, George Arthur Crump, insisted on the following parameters in the design: (1) no hole should be laid out parallel to the next, (2) no more than two consecutive holes should play in the same direction, (3) players shouldn't be able to see any hole other than the one they are playing, and (4) the layout should require the player to use every club in the bag.

Well, back to our friend, the head pro at the local muni. **He's caught in a tough situation.** There have been too many new golf courses added in the Salt Lake area in the last 10 to 15 years, and this has happened despite the fact that golf participation has actually declined. Meanwhile our golf pro's operating expenses have kept going up while his revenues have gone done. The course itself, as well as the clubhouse and other facilities, are showing the effects of deferred maintenance. And there is little, if any, opportunity for him to increase green fees. In fact, golf courses in our area (both municipal and public) are in heavy competition with each other and are offering significant discounts to attract more golfers. The bottom line? **It's a great time to be a golfer and a difficult time to be the one running a golf course.**

I'm optimistic that the golf industry will bounce back and that in a few years things will turn around for many of the golf courses that are struggling. In the meantime, **let's remember to give our local golf pros a big thanks and tell them how much we appreciate them and their course.**

Golf Term

Grain

In 1607, Shakespeare used the phrase "go against the grain" in his play Coriolanus. It was one of the earliest uses of the term and was intended to mean something that is contrary to a person's natural tendency or inclination. **In golf, grain refers to the direction that the grass grows or lies on a green.**

Since grain can affect the speed and direction that a golf ball will roll, a golfer who wants to putt well needs to determine the grain, if any, of the grass and then:

- Stroke the ball a little harder than otherwise when putting against the grain
- Hit the ball a little softer when the putt is with the grain
- Adjust the aim of the putt when going across the grain, remembering that the ball will tend to break towards the direction the grain is growing

20

Mission Hills 216 in China

When I first lived in Hong Kong some 50 years ago, **Hong Kong was a British Crown Colony** and it had two golf courses, one on the island and one in the New Territories. I don't recall knowing of any golf courses located in Mainland China at that time. Under the rule of Chairman Mao, the Chinese viewed golf as **an evil bourgeois pastime** and they steered clear of it. In fact, the government banned it.

When we went back to Hong Kong in 2006 to live there for three years, things had changed. Hong Kong had been handed back to China by the British, and China was into golf big time. Hong Kong itself had seven golf courses and **the largest golf complex in the entire world sat just over the Hong Kong border in Shenzhen, China.** That golf complex is called **Mission Hills 216** and I have been fortunate enough to play it twice – once on the Olazabol course and once on the Els course.

Mission Hills is amazing. **It consists of 12 full–sized courses all in one location.** The beautiful courses have been designed by an array of famous golf personalities – **Olazabol, Els, Palmer, Nicklaus, Dye, Faldo, etc.** The central club house, one of three clubhouses in the complex, is a spectacular 300,000 square foot show place with the largest pro shop in the world. The courses are well–groomed, the staff is extremely friendly, and if you didn't know any better you'd think you were golfing at a premier country club in the U.S. Mission Hills has a five–star resort hotel, a world–class spa, a huge top–of–the–line shopping mall, and the largest tennis center in Asia.

Because golf was brought to China from other countries, and because China uses characters for their written language rather than an alphabet, the word "golf" and the words associated with playing golf don't exist in their language. **So they have transliterated those words.** That means they have chosen sounds from their language and have used those sounds to approximate the English way of saying the word. They do this all the time with foreign words that don't exist in Chinese. Here are some examples of transliterated golf words in the Cantonese Chinese language that have been spelled out in what is called Romanization. (Cantonese is the dialect spoken in Hong Kong.)

- **Golf** – Gōyíhfū
- **Ball** – Bō
- **Birdie** – Bōdí
- **Caddie** – Gàdí
- **Cup** – Kàp

Today, China is struggling with golf as a pastime. **They can't quite make up their mind about it.** When the Communist government came into power in 1949, they banned all golf courses saying it was the sport of millionaires. That lasted until the 1980s when the ban was lifted and the first new course was built in 1984 in Guangdong Province. As China became a world power and the people began having more spending money and leisure time, the country built lots of golf courses and many Chinese citizens, especially Chinese businessmen, became passionate about golf. Playing golf became quite a status symbol. Then in 2004, a moratorium was placed on building golf courses in China. **The government said the ban was aimed at saving water, reducing pollution from fertilizers and pesticides, and "protecting the collective land of the peasants."** However, courses continued to be built and opened, mostly as part of China's real estate boom, and China now has well over 600 golf courses. **Over the past decade, no country in the world has built more golf courses than China.**

Many of the new courses were snuck in under the radar. Golf course builders ignored the ban and got creative, making sure the course was part of a large real estate development that helped disguise the golf course. **They avoided using the term golf in the name of the development** and often indicated on their plans that those large open spaces around which their new houses were being built were simply green space, an ecological reserve, or a special activities park.

At the present time China is caught in a dilemma. Officially they don't approve of golf, but unofficially they love the sport and are very, very proud of the fact that several Chinese golfers are achieving some prominence in golf. Both on the women's tour and the men's tour, a few Chinese are moving up the world rankings.

In fact, Shanshan Feng won the LPGA Championship in 2012 and is a multiple winner on the women's tour. She is ranked as one of the top 10 women golfers in the world. And China, which hosted the Beijing Summer Olympics in 2008, loves the Olympics and the exposure it gives their nation. They have a zeal for wanting to excel in all sports and now that golf has been added to the Olympics they want to make sure they field a world–class golf team for the competition.

The Mission Hills 216 development in Shenzhen has been hugely successful, and despite the official ban on golf in the country, **another Mission Hills complex is being built on Hainan Island,** which is located off the southeastern coast of China. Hainan has volcanic mountains, beautiful beaches, and is the only tropical island in China. Besides multiple golf courses, Mission Hills Hainan has an 18–story resort hotel, many restaurants, lots of shopping – and, get this, **168 natural hot and cold mineral spring pools.** Sounds to me like a great place to spend some time.

Golf Term

Par

Pretty much everyone knows what par means in golf. **Par is the number of strokes a good golfer is expected to take on any given hole – or on all 18 holes combined.** You'd think the word had been used around golf courses pretty much from the beginning, but par actually didn't come into golf usage until the late 1800s. From the identical word in Latin, **par, meaning equality,** is found in words such as parity, partner, and parallel. A phrase such as "on a par" means of equal value or on the same level.

An interesting thing about using the word par in phrases related to golf is that **in golf we use it backwards.** When we say that a golfer is under par, that is good; but when we talk about a sick person and say that they are feeling below par or subpar, that is not good.

I wonder if that has anything to do with the fact that golf is kind of a backwards sport when it comes to scoring. **To my knowledge, golf is the only sport using a ball in which the low score wins.** In all other ball sports, the high score wins.

21

Playing by Whose Rules?

"Golf is a game in which you yell 'fore,' shoot six, and write down five." – Paul Harvey

My round of golf at the Old Mill golf course had been very relaxing and enjoyable. Early in the morning I had walked up as a single player, and the starter was kind enough to get me out quite quickly with three pleasant gentlemen – **Rich, Dan, and Alan** (I have changed their names). Old Mill is a wonderful municipal course with a terrific view located on Salt Lake City's east bench. Because I can drive there from my home in just a few minutes, I go there quite often when I don't have plans to play with some of my regular golfing buddies.

Rich, Dan, and Alan told me that they play golf together about twice a week and that they like to play at different courses in the area rather than go to the same one all the time. They all are quite good recreational golfers. **The thing that was interesting to me about the group was how creative they were with their scoring.** They had developed a way of playing golf that took quite a few liberties with the rules. But they absolutely enjoyed the round and were not the least bit concerned that they didn't play according to the official Rules of Golf. **They had their own method and style of golf and they loved it.** They were just out having a good time with friends.

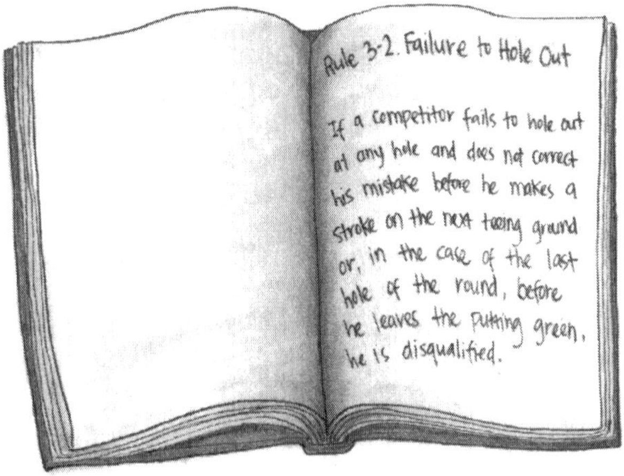

After the round and after they had driven out of the parking lot, I sat down at a table on one of the clubhouse's patios. I took out some paper and pen and made notes while I thought about what their true scores would have been had they adhered strictly to all golf rules. Rich had given himself a 94 for the round, Dan wrote down 97, and Alan carded a 98.

Here are a few of my observations about their round – and please remember that I am in no way an expert on golf rules:

1. **There were more than a dozen of golf's 34 rules violated during the round, some of them quite a few times.** In saying this, I don't wish to infer that they were cheating, instead they were just trying to make their golf experience more enjoyable. Each of them did what they did with the full knowledge, approval, and encouragement of their playing partners.
2. The group would have incurred **quite a few penalty strokes** had they adhered to the rules – and by quite a few I mean something on the order of 30 to 40 extra strokes

among the three of them.

3. Had the rules been strictly applied, **each one of them would have been disqualified nearly a half–dozen times.** (Certain violations of the rules, of course, require a golfer to be disqualified rather than just to receive penalty strokes.)

Among the most common violations I observed were:

Improperly Moving the Ball

A basic tenet of golf is that **we must play the ball where it lies.** There are certain instances in which we are allowed to move the ball or take a drop, but we are not permitted to do things such as kick our ball out of the rough, remove it from a divot, or move it out of a sand trap with our hand. **Rule 18 (Ball at Rest Moved)** says that when a player's ball is in play, if the player lifts or moves it or causes it to move except as permitted within the rules, the player incurs a penalty of one stroke. This particular group of golfers moved their golf balls a lot and would have incurred many penalty strokes had they been sticking to the real rules.

Sharing Information and Advice

Although as friends we love to help each other out, under **Rule 8 (Advice; Indicating Line of Play)**, no one except a player's caddie may give advice of any kind to the golfer during the round of play. Our group was continually talking with each other about such things as which club to use, where the hazards and tricky parts of the course are located, and how a particular putt was going to break. **All of this sharing of information and advice is prohibited and results in penalty strokes under the rules.** (Sharing information and advice with your playing partner is, of course, allowed if you are playing match play. Match play is the format used during competitions such as the Ryder Cup.)

Mulligans

All three of them took several mulligans as they hit their tee shots on various holes. Rather than have to play a difficult second shot after a really lousy first shot, they just got out a new ball and hit another drive. No one objected. It was understood by the group that sooner or later they all would mess up a drive, so why let that ruin an otherwise good round? A second drive, of course, is sometimes allowed under the rules, but you can't count it as your first stroke on that hole as they did, per **Rule 27 (Ball Lost or Out of Bounds; Provisional Ball).** So when they took a mulligan, they failed to recognize that that was their third stroke, not their first. As the crusty old British caddie was quoted as saying, **"Sir, that's not a mulligan, that's a three."**

Failure to Hole Out

Rule 3 (Stroke Play) informs us that if a competitor fails to hole out on any hole and does not correct the mistake before they hit their drive on the next hole, they are disqualified. **Every time they gave each other a gimme putt and did not hole out, they disqualified themselves and technically did not have a score for that hole.** Among the three of them, this happened at least a dozen times during the round.

Trying out Someone Else's Club

And here's a tough rule to keep when we're out with friends for a fun round. We all love to let others in our group try out our new driver, iron, or putter – but that is definitely taboo under the rules. A player is allowed a maximum of 14 clubs in the bag. Even if you have fewer than 14 in your bag at the start of play, under **Rule 4 (Clubs)** you are not allowed to add or borrow any club selected for play by any other person playing on the course. **So, for instance, when Alan let Rich use his new driver on the 12th tee, they both incurred a penalty.**

Other Violations

Our group also broke the rules by hitting a moving ball before it stopped (twice), marking and replacing the ball in an improper manner on the green (many times), teeing off outside of the tee markers (once), grounding the club in a hazard (several times), and cleaning mud off the ball while out in a fairway or rough (three times that I observed).

Even though I was aware of their bending of the rules, I really enjoyed playing golf with Rich, Dan, and Alan. We had a good time together and I was especially happy to see these three nice men having so much fun on a gorgeous day on a beautiful golf course. And I'm guessing that if they had one message for the rest of us **it would be to encourage us to loosen up a bit out there** and to not worry so much about the rules so we can more fully enjoy, appreciate, and treasure our golfing experiences together.

"Go out and have fun. Golf is a game for everyone, not just for the talented few." – Harvey Penick

Golf Term

Sweet Spot

The old wooden persimmon drivers of the past had quite a small sweet spot – **often not much larger than the size of a pea.** Today's metal drivers are designed to have a much larger sweet spot – **sometimes nearly as large as the golf ball itself.**

The sweet spot on a golf club (on drivers, irons, as well as on putters) is the location on the face of the club where your swing achieves the maximum response. It is the spot that makes the ball go the farthest. In technical terms, as stated in Wikipedia:

> "It is the spot at which the ball absorbs the maximum amount of the available forward momentum and rebounds away from the club with a greater velocity than if struck at any other point on the club."

Hitting the sweet spot maximizes the golf shot. The pros are experts at hitting that spot on the club nearly every time they swing. The rest of us? It is something we work on continually.

With today's large drivers, the sweet spot is not necessarily in the exact center of the club face. The sweet spot is usually in the center of the club horizontally (meaning from the heel to the toe of the club face), **but vertically it may be a little bit above the center of the face.** This is because as the clubs have gotten bigger, the center of gravity has moved farther back in the club. This has moved the sweet spot higher on the face.

22

The Road Less Traveled

One of the nice aspects of cruising is that there are many different ways for passengers to spend their time while their ship is in port for the day – including playing golf. One of my own favorite days on shore was in the **Falkland Islands** while my wife and I were on a cruise that took us around the southern tip of South America. The experience I had there reminded me of Robert Frost's poem ***The Road Not Taken***. Concerning the two roads that diverged in a yellow wood, he wrote,

> **"I took the one less traveled by,**
> **And that made all the difference."**

Before we left on our cruise, we carefully went over the various shore excursions offered by the cruise line in each port of call on the trip. There were eight stops on the itinerary. **A total of 54 possible shore excursions were offered** – an average of nearly seven per port. The prices of the shore excursions ranged from **$27 per person on the low end** (a short city tour in Montevideo, Uruguay) **to $2,999 per person on the high end** (an airplane flight to Antarctica for a day's visit to a research station there).

After reviewing what was available, we signed up for a number of shore excursions before we left home. However, when it came to our stop in the Falkland Islands, we decided to keep our morning there open and to just do something on our own.

Upon going ashore in Port Stanley, the capital city of the Falkland Islands, we split up. My wife looked around the quaint village and went shopping **while I decided to see if the golf course that had been built by British soldiers in the 1930s was still there.**

Not knowing where to go, I found an elderly local man on the dock and asked him about the golf course. He looked to me to be an honest and safe person and he invited me to get into his car and proceeded to give me a lift to the course, which was a little ways outside of the city. He chuckled when I told him I wanted to play golf there, and when we arrived at the course after driving down a bumpy rural road, I understood why he laughed. What once was a nice golf course built on the side of a beautiful hill overlooking the South Atlantic Ocean was now a nearly–abandoned site with **overgrown fairways and, shall we say, some interesting greens.**

As mentioned previously, whenever I travel I take with me a small cloth bag with several golf balls, some tees, some golf ball markers, and a golf glove. I then rent clubs when I get to the course. Well, this course's pro shop was a little brown wooden building with all of the doors and windows locked. Cut into one of the exterior walls was a small slot. Next to the slot was a sign that said, **"Honesty Box."** This was apparently where you were to pay for using the course. I was about to give up on playing golf there when I noticed **several old golf clubs lying in the grass** a few feet to the side of the club house. Not seeing anyone around, and with my ride having already returned to Port Stanley, I slid some money into the Honesty Box slot and decided to give the course a try.

Several hours later I was glad that I had chosen **the road less traveled** during our visit to the Falkland Islands. **My quirky round of golf there had been wonderful!** By trial and error I had discovered that the course had 18 tees but only 12 greens. Six of the greens were used twice. The weather during my round had been pleasant, the scenery spectacular, and I was able to play as many balls as I wanted without worrying about holding up anyone else on the course – because there was no one else in sight.

As I left the course and took a leisurely stroll back to town, I was smiling. I never would have imagined that I would play golf in the Falkland Islands. Even today, just thinking about it makes me chuckle. As I got back to town I had lunch in a charming local eatery and then met up with my wife for our late afternoon shore excursion to visit some historic battlefields.

I am grateful that on that beautiful morning in the Falkland Islands I took **the road less traveled – a road that made all the difference on that day.**

(Note – This was first published in the author's book ***Cruising – A View Through the Porthole.***)

Golf Term

Waggle

The golf pro and his friends in the pro shop were laughing really hard. The pro had just told his friends about what had happened as he gave a first golf lesson to an older gentleman. The man just wasn't getting the hang of hitting the ball, **so the pro suggested that he might try a little waggle just before attempting the swing.** The gentleman misunderstood him, and just before his next try at hitting the ball, **he waddled.**

To waggle is to make a slight swinging movement back and forth with the club head just prior to the swing. Some golfers like to do this to keep their arms and legs relaxed and to get their body ready to hit the ball. Jason Dufner is probably the prime example of a current golfer who waggles his club before he hits the ball. Another proponent of the waggle is Tom Watson. He likes to waggle the club before he starts his swing in order to establish good rhythm and avoid tension.

To waddle, of course, is what ducks and Charlie Chaplin do as they walk. It means to shuffle one's feet back and forth in short little steps. Trying to hit a golf ball while waddling is really difficult to do and is not recommended.

Inside the Floating Green

The waitress just brought out my entrée – **grilled wild sockeye salmon.** It has been seared with huckleberry barbecue sauce and is accompanied by jasmine rice and grilled vegetables. Delicious! On a beautiful and calm evening in late summer with the sun beginning to set, **I am sitting outdoors on the patio of the Floating Green Restaurant in Coeur d'Alene, Idaho.** Between bites, I find myself thinking about an interesting and unusual experience I had earlier in the day on a "boat" I can see floating in front of me out in the lake. The "boat" I am talking about is the famous moveable floating green at the Coeur d'Alene Resort Golf Course in northern Idaho.

Have you been there? Have you played that beautiful golf course and tried your hand at teeing off on their **renowned par–3 14th hole** with the floating green? Were you able to land your tee shot on the green and get it to stay there? (Per local rule, you only get two tries.) Have you gone on their little boat, named the Putter, which takes you from the tee box out to the green after you've hit your tee shot? **If not, I highly recommend this experience to you.** I can assure you it will be a memorable one.

Having made prior arrangements, I traveled to Coeur d'Alene

and met **Kevin Hicks,** the golf course superintendent, and **Andy MacKimmie,** the head golf pro and director of marketing, one morning at 8:00 a.m. at the beautiful club house. They showed me into a conference room where we talked for a while about their golf course and the famous floating green. I had lots of questions for them and they were most gracious in answering them. We then took a short stroll to the 14th tee and boarded a small maintenance boat to visit the green. What was unusual was that we were not going out to go on top of the green. **Instead, we were heading out to go inside the green.**

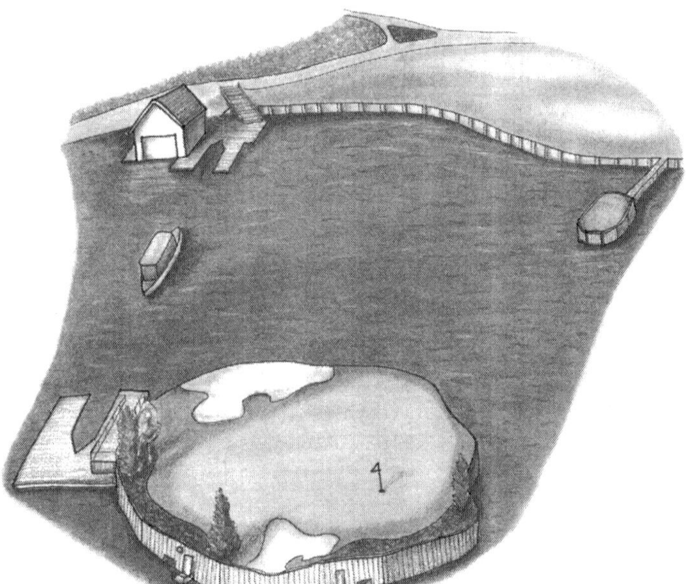

Our boat maneuvered around the right side of the green and tied up at a docking area at the rear where there was a little access door that allowed us to go **inside the green.** After unlocking the door, we squeezed into a small control room. A control room? **Why does a green need a control room?** Because this green is like a boat in that it can be moved to change how far away it is from the tee. **The control room contains the motors, cables, levers, and gauges that operate the green.** Kevin and Andy showed me the green's intricate support structure and explained what is involved in moving this floating island. Basically, to change the green you move a dial on a panel to the yardage desired and then push a button that activates the various electric motors.

When we were done there we hopped back on the little boat and returned to shore so I could make the 10:40 a.m. tee time they had set up for me. I then spent the rest of the morning and most of the afternoon playing golf at their gorgeous course. **It is a stunningly beautiful one with vibrant green grass, thousands of red geraniums, and some terrific golf holes.** And one of my favorite things was a complimentary sports massage that is given to each golfer before they tee off on the first hole. After the round, I rested up for a few hours and then had time in the evening for a leisurely dinner at the Floating Green Restaurant that overlooks the lake and the green.

Concerning the floating green, some of the things I learned from Kevin, Andy, and others were:

- **How the Idea Came About** – Prior to it being a golf course, the land was an old logging operation and saw mill. As **Duane Hagadone** was walking the property he had purchased in the late 1980s and was imagining the concept of the course, he saw an old log barge sitting out in the lake a little ways from shore. He suggested to his golf course architect, Scott Miller, that they **put a green on top of a barge like that.** When Scott mentioned that it would probably be very costly, Mr. Hagadone said that it didn't matter because he wanted to create something significant and new in the golf industry – and something with some sizzle. And that he did! And although Mr. Hagadone has never disclosed the cost of building the green, he says that it is the most expensive one ever built anywhere in the world – probably by at least three times.
- **Nautical Engineer's Help** – A few weeks after my trip to Coeur d'Alene, I was able to visit on the phone with the course architect, Scott Miller, about the design of the green. Among other things, **he said that he enlisted the**

help of a nautical engineer from Seattle in the design process because the green was like a large boat that needed to meet several criteria: (1) it needed to be movable, (2) it had to be stable enough not to rock and roll when the lake was choppy so that golfers wouldn't be moving up and down and sideways as they putted, and (3) it had to be able to support 12 inches of soil, another 4 inches of top dressing, grass, trees, and flowers. Since this kind of a project had never been done before and there was no template for it, the design process was complex, requiring specialized engineering. Concrete cells and polystyrene foam blocks were used to make up the basic support structure and then the green itself was built on top of that. The weight of the 15,000–square–foot finished product varies greatly with the amount of moisture on it, with usually about half of the island green being above water level and half below.

- **How it Moves** – Four 7/8–inch cables wound around four large metals spools that are located in the control room inside the green move the green forward and backward. Two cables come out underwater from the front of the green and are anchored close to shore and two come out from the rear and are anchored further out into the lake. **When activated, electrical motors rotate the spools, allowing the cables to simultaneously shorten in the front and lengthen in the rear to move the green towards shore.** The process is reversed to increase the distance from the tee to the green. Kevin and Andy said that the possible range from shore is from 95 to 270 yards with the typical distance they set being about 130 to 180 yards.
- **A Green Green** – The floating green is ecologically green. **An umbilical cord runs under the water along the bottom of the lake from the shore to the green.** It brings water and electricity to the green and returns all used water back to the shore for filtration and disposal. None of the irrigation water, fertilizer, or other nutrients

used to keep the green and its landscaping growing runs off into the lake. All of it is contained, recaptured at the green, and pumped back to shore for handling so as not to pollute the lake.

- **The Coast Guard** – The little boat, the Putter, that takes the golfers out to the green after they've hit their tee shots **falls under the regulation of the U. S. Coast Guard** because it carries what they consider to be commercial public passengers. Periodically, the Coast Guard inspects the boat to make sure it is safe and that those who operate it are properly trained.
- **Leased Rights** – Both the floating green and the driving range are located out in the lake (floating golf balls are used at the driving range). The golf course, **through a lease agreement with the State of Idaho,** has obtained permission to use these portions of the lake for a fee. (The southern one-third of the lake is owned by the Coeur d'Alene Indian tribe and the northern part of the lake where the golf course sits is owned by the state.)

Well, I've just finished eating the excellent salmon dish. Now I've got a tough decision to make. **Should I have the triple chocolate brownie sundae, the bread pudding, or the cinnamon apple cream pie to finish off the meal?** I think I'll go for the sundae. That will be a wonderful way to bring an end to a most interesting day where I was able to go **inside the floating green** and play golf at the Coeur d'Alene Golf Resort.

Oh, and I should disclose that I missed both of my tries to get my tee shot onto the floating green. Today's yardage from the blue tees was 174. My first ball was a few yards short and my second one missed the green to the left. I don't feel too badly about this though because Kevin and Andy estimate that about half of all golfers miss the green on both tries – and even Clint Eastwood missed it when he golfed here a few years ago. His two shots were short, after which he quipped that he needed a bit more ammo.

I guess I'd better plan on coming back to Coeur d'Alene

another time so I can try again. I'm certainly not going to let that hole get the best of me – **and I'd also like to try the jalapeno encrusted trout drizzled with a lemon caper sauce that is listed on the restaurant's menu.**

Golf Term

Yips

Oh the dreaded yips! Yips is a term that refers to a twitching or jittery movement disorder that some golfers experience when trying to sink a short putt. The yips is thought to be mostly a psychological condition – but it may also be a fine motor skill problem. **The origin of the word as it relates to golf is uncertain, but the term has been around golf for many years.**

And it does not only apply to golf. If you are a dart player with the problem, it is called **dartitis.** An archer calls it **target panic.** And even bowlers in cricket, pitchers in baseball, and free–throw shooters in basketball experience the yips.

The cause? Unknown. The solution? It's anyone's guess. Athletes affected by the condition are usually older and very experienced in their sport. Suddenly without explanation they suffer a loss of their previous skills. Sometimes an athlete will recover their ability, but often they can never quite get back to their earlier level of expertise.

I believe it was comedian George Carlin who joked that there is only one sure way to get rid of the yips in golf – **and that way is to give up the game and take up bowling or bingo.**

24

Trees are 90% Air? Baloney!

I think Mr. Grandy would have been proud of me. Mr. Grandy, my 11th grade science teacher at Highland High School, spent the year teaching us the importance of the scientific method. He lectured on it, tested us on it, made us write essays on it, and had us use the scientific method in everything we did in his class. It's due to Mr. Grandy and the scientific method that I know how to build a super neat volcano using baking soda, vinegar, dish washing soap, yellow and red dye, newspaper, flour, water – and one of Mom's Tupperware bowls.

When golfing, whenever my drive goes off the fairway, as it is wont to do, and lands so that there is a tree between my ball and the green, my good old golfing buddies joke with me that **there is nothing to worry about because trees are 90% air.** So even though I should know better by now, I often succumb to their urging and take a chance by trying to hit that little old white sphere through the tree. **Sadly, I've found that that is a great way to add a couple of unnecessary strokes to my score.**

Well, back to the scientific method. During the writing of this book, I wanted to find out for myself what the impact of a tree was on a golf ball. **I decided to conduct a scientific experiment,** à la

Mr. Grandy's teachings. So I did the following:

First – Formulate a question

- Can a golf ball go through a tree?

Second – Form an explanatory hypothesis

- It can, but probably not as often as you think.

Third – Test the hypothesis

- Early one morning I went to a golf course near our home and found a medium–sized deciduous tree (a tree that has leaves) off to one side of a par–4 fairway. I set myself up about 20 yards behind the tree so that the tree was directly in line with the green and then **I hit 100 balls at the green,** trying to go through the tree with each ball.

Fourth – Analyze the data

- Here are the results of my scientific experiment:
    - **2** – Number of balls that went through the tree without hitting any part of the tree.
    - **20** – Number of balls that hit some part of the tree but continued toward the green.
    - **38** – Number of balls that got through the tree but had a significant change of direction and velocity as a result of hitting some part of the tree.
    - **31** – Number of balls that were pretty much stopped dead by the tree.
    - **9** – Number of balls that hit some part of the tree and bounced back near me or ended up behind me.

Fifth – Interpret the data and draw conclusions

- Here are a few things I learned:
    - My golf buddies are doofuses for daring me to hit through trees.
    - Even if a tree is 90% air, so what? The real question is, "Is there a straight unobstructed path through the tree that is large enough for a golf ball? And am I a good enough golfer to find that path?"
    - Trees may be 90% air but they are 100% trouble.
    - About 20% of the branches and leaves block 80% of the shots.

- Is it my imagination, or do leaves and branches actually have the ability to jump in front of your golf ball when they want to?

Clair, my friend at our local nursery, has been in the tree and plant business for over 40 years. He is a walking encyclopedia of trees – and he's also a golfer. I asked Clair about trees and golf and he reminded me why golf course architects plant trees on golf courses. Their purposes are: (1) to separate holes so as to provide privacy and protection, (2) to frame holes so as to provide backdrops to greens, (3) to beautify the golf course, and **(4) to be a hazard to golfers and to penalize players who can't keep their golf ball in the fairway.**

In conclusion, the sixth step of the scientific method, per Mr. Grandy, is to publish the results – hence this chapter in the book. And while I'm in the process of publishing, let me take the opportunity to share with you my first ever golf poem, with apologies to Joyce Kilmer who wrote "Trees."

Trees are 90% Air? Baloney!
By Lee H. Van Dam

I think that I shall never see,
A golf course tree allowing me,
To hit my shot right through the crown,
'Cause it will knock my ball right down.

I hit my drive, and it goes right,
Oh, woe is me, the rough's my plight,
To make it worse, just straight ahead,
Stands a large oak tree with a great big spread.

My buddies say, "No need to fear,
Going through the tree is usually clear."
"It's mostly air, just give it a try."
So I go for it – then wonder why.

I've golfed enough, I ought to learn,
Tree shots are something I should spurn,
So now I add my own testimony,
Trees are 90% air? Baloney!

Golf Term

Whiff

Going back to the 1500s in Scotland, **a wheff was something crooked, askew, off course, or off–center.** It didn't take long for golfers to start using the term whenever someone's swing was off course enough to completely miss the ball. As the years went by, the common spelling of the word was changed to **whiff.**

Certainly one of the most embarrassing things in golf is **a whiff**. **That's when you carefully set yourself up for the perfect shot, take a mighty swing at the ball – and miss it completely.** The penalty? Per the Rules of Golf, you must count the swing as a stroke. **The rule is: If you swing at your ball with the intent to hit it, it is a shot regardless of whether you make contact.** This applies on the tee, out in the fairway, in the rough, or even on the green.

25

My Personal Favorites

As a society we love to rate things. We have Nielsen ratings for TV, Michelin ratings for restaurants, Consumer Report ratings for consumer products, and the MPAA ratings for movies. **I decided to do some ratings myself, so here are two of my personal ratings lists.** The first shows my ten favorite golf courses that I have played. As I began working on this list, I simply started writing down the golf courses I have enjoyed playing. **Wow! I ended up with quite a long list because there are so many wonderful golf courses.** Narrowing it down to just ten was not easy to do, but here is what I ended up with:

My Ten Favorite Courses to Play

1. Hobble Creek Golf Course, Springville, Utah
2. The Old Course at St. Andrews, Scotland
3. Coeur d'Alene Resort Golf Course, Coeur d'Alene, Idaho
4. Pebble Beach Golf Links, Pebble Beach, California
5. Tour 18 Golf Course, Houston, Texas
6. Wolf Creek Golf Club, Mesquite, Nevada
7. Mission Hills 216 Golf Club, Olazabol Course, Shenzhen,

China
8. Wasatch Mountain State Park, Midway, Utah
9. Woodstock Country Club, Woodstock, Vermont
10. Old Mill Golf Course, Salt Lake City, Utah

Then I started thinking about my golf experiences, not just about the courses I have played. **Sometimes golf experiences are broader and richer than just the golf itself.** As with the above list, my favorite experiences totaled much more than ten. But here is the final list:

My Ten Favorite Golf Experiences

1. Playing the Old Course at St. Andrews, Scotland
2. Playing Pebble Beach Golf Links in California
3. Participating in the Midnight Madness golf tournament in Yellowknife, Canada
4. The last round of golf where my father was with me on a golf course. At age 89, Dad drove the cart and watched me play.
5. The road less traveled round of golf in the Falkland Islands
6. Jumping off a tour bus to play golf in Tahiti. I had not planned to play golf that day, but when our bus went by a beautiful course, I asked the bus driver to stop so I could hop off. He obliged. I told my wife I would somehow meet her back at the hotel later in the day – and then I walked over to the course and played golf in Tahiti! Afterwards I hitchhiked back, riding in the rear of an old pickup truck to the hotel.
7. Playing the Royal Nepal Golf Club in Kathmandu, Nepal
8. Playing Golfclub Old Course Loenen in The Netherlands
9. Playing Mission Hills 216 in Shenzhen, China
10. Writing this book about golf

As I reflect on these lists and on all of the golfing I have done, I feel like Hardy Greaves in the movie, *The Legend of*

Bagger Vance. In the movie, Rannulph Junuh, a promising young golfer played by Matt Damon, is talking to Hardy Greaves, Bagger Vance's young assistant played by J. Michael Moncrief. Here is a portion of their conversation:

Rannulph: "You really love this game, don't you?"
Hardy: **"It's the greatest game there is."**
Rannulph: "You really think so?"
Hardy: **"Ask anybody. It's fun. It's hard and you stand out there on that green, green grass, and it's just you and the ball and there ain't nobody to beat up on but yourself. There just ain't no other game like it."**

I am grateful for the sport of golf, and for golf courses, and for golf friends, and for many wonderful golf experiences. **"It's the greatest game there is. There just ain't no other game like it."**

Golf Term

Tin Cup

A tin cup is a golfer who has a weakness for repeatedly going for (and often missing) difficult golf shots. In the popular 1996 golf movie, *Tin Cup*, Kevin Costner starred as Roy McAvoy, a washed up golf pro whose nickname is **Tin Cup.** Roy's game is good, but his head is the problem. He makes it into the U. S. Open and is in position to tie for a playoff spot with a par if he hits the safe shot by laying up in front of the pond that sits in front of the 18th green. **Roy chooses the risky shot instead and goes for the green.** The ball lands on the putting surface and then trickles back into the water. Roy asks his caddy for another ball and it ends up with the same result – in the water. Roy won't give up and finally with the last ball left in his bag, he hits it over the pond, onto the green, and into the hole – **for a 12.** Golfers who attempt risky shots instead of playing it safe are called tin cups.

About the Author

Born in Salt Lake City, Utah, Lee H. Van Dam has also lived in The Netherlands and Hong Kong. He holds an MBA degree and is the owner of a real estate management, sales, and consulting firm.

Lee and his wife, Holly, are the parents of two children, and they have seven grandchildren. They love to travel and Lee enjoys playing golf. His first book is titled ***Cruising – A View Through the Porthole.***